The MAP CORNER

Good Year Books

are available for preschool through grade 12 and for every basic curriculum subject plus many enrichment areas. For more Good Year Books, contact your local bookseller or educational dealer. For a complete catalog with information about other Good Year Books, please write:

Good Year Books
Department GYB
1900 East Lake Avenue
Glenview, Illinois 60025

The MAP CORNER

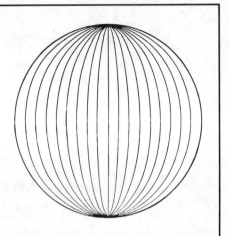

Arnold B. Cheyney
Professor of Education
University of Miami

Donald L. Capone
Professor of Geography
University of Miami, Coral Gables

Scott, Foresman and Company
Glenview, Illinois   Dallas, Texas
Oakland, New Jersey   Palo Alto, California
Tucker, Georgia   London

Illustrations in Explorer Narratives and "Maps: Their Makers and Users" by Jeanne Cheyney.

ISBN: 0-673-16615-5

16 15 14 13 12   EBI   96 95 94 93

Preface

The Map Corner is for teachers and students in elementary and junior high schools. The book is meant to be duplicated and used creatively. It is a supplement to existing programs. The reference materials found in most classrooms and libraries, such as globes, reference maps, encyclopedias, and other materials, can be used more fully with *The Map Corner*.

The Map Corner has one major purpose: to help boys and girls develop the concept of location. Other map skills are developed, but they are meant to amplify the major purpose of location.

The activities suggested in *The Map Corner* should be used to fit the abilities of individual students. Therefore, some activities may need to be modified.

The Authors

Acknowledgments

The authors are grateful to the following persons and firms for their help in finding materials, providing counsel, and giving permission to publish their materials.

Jeanne S. Cheyney, School of Education and Allied Professions, University of Miami, for the pen and ink illustrations throughout the text portion of the book.

Wanda J. Williams, Reference Librarian, Richter Library, University of Miami, for help in library searches.

Dr. Charles E. Hannemann and Dr. Eugene F. Provenzo, Jr., School of Education and Allied Professions, University of Miami, for suggestions and help in library searches.

Dr. Rita Bornstein, Assistant Vice President for Development Affairs, University of Miami, and Kathleen A. Shea, Director of the National Sex Equity Demonstration Project for information on women explorers.

Gerald A. Petersen, Associate Director, National Weather Service, United States Department of Commerce, National Oceanic and Atmospheric Administration, for supplying information on hurricanes and thunderstorms.

Edward M. Storin and Rick Brownlee, *The Miami Herald,* for permission to include Appendix Map 22, Monarch Butterfly Migration. *Reprinted by permission from The Miami Herald, Wednesday, June 24, 1981.*

The National Audubon Society for the adaptation of Appendix Map 30, Bird Migration Routes. *Used by permission, The National Audubon Society.*

Our thanks also to the airlines, railroads, bus lines, and Library of Congress who supplied materials that stimulated us to consider more nontraditional approaches to map skill development.

The Authors

Contents

Introduction

The Map Corner will only have achieved its purpose when teachers have taken it apart and duplicated and used its material creatively to help students become more familiar with their world. We created this book to help classroom teachers in a practical way. We believe, too, that it is a book that goes beyond the limits of helpfulness in the traditional social studies sense because map skills are as much a part of a reading skills program as they are social studies.

Purpose of The Map Corner

The major purpose of The Map Corner is to help students develop the skill of locating places on the earth. Before a rational discussion about problems affecting people can begin, students must know where an event has occurred. With instant communication to every hamlet, town, and city on the globe, all of us are becoming aware that the smallest incident anywhere can affect us all.

A Cafeteria of Map Skills. The Map Corner is designed as a cafeteria of map skill exercises rather than as a sequential program of study or a progression of skills, with one building on another. The reality of a classroom filled with students is that each person is at a different skill level; hence, there is a need to choose materials that fit the abilities and levels of individuals and groups.

Reference Materials Necessary. First, classrooms that use The Map Corner must have access to globes, classroom maps, atlases, and encyclopedias. These are the basics for any map skill program. Second, students must have some knowledge of how to use reference skills or be in the process of learning how to use them. The lessons and activities in The Map Corner, as with other materials of this nature, can only supplement these mainstays.

How to Use the Map Corner

Lesson Plans

The lesson plans in The Map Corner are designed to start teachers and their classes on an exciting learning experience. While they do contain objectives, teachers may choose to formulate their own. The interests and needs of students vary and these interests and needs must be paramount when planning for children.

Reading materials necessary for the lesson can often be duplicated from the lesson plan itself. Reference materials are often found in classrooms or in the school library. The appendix maps, of course, can be duplicated. There are times when students may bring reference materials from home. The Procedures are to be used individually, with small groups, or with full class participation. The Evaluation Activities are left to teachers' discretion because the lessons are meant to be adapted to various levels of interest and abilities.

In using the lesson plans, teachers are encouraged to add or delete material to make them useful to students.

The pages in The Map Corner are easily removed and converted to a duplicating master in a master-making thermal heat unit. The pages themselves can be photocopied intact from the book or removed and inserted in other texts or lesson plan books for later use.

The maps and articles in the Explorer Series and the Map Activity Quizzes make excellent skill and enrichment material for interest centers, for use in lesson plans, for supplementary reading when studying history and geography, and for use in understanding current events at local, state, national, and international levels. For instance, the first thing students need to ask themselves when a major news event takes place is, "Where is it?" Their second response should be; "Let's find it on the map." An understanding of the importance of an event can only come about when the basic information of location is known.

Certificate of Map Skill Proficiency

Most teachers do not have the time to conduct an intensive map skill program as part of their curriculum, nor do many have the background in geography to feel comfortable teaching one. Therefore, *The Map Corner* has a number of activity quizzes that students can do individually on their own. As these are completed, the teacher can check the quizzes for general correctness and accuracy. The Map Activity Quiz Checklist (Appendix Map 2) can be duplicated and used by the teacher as a record of each student's progress.

Certificates (Appendix Map 1) are issued whenever a student has acquired a particular map skill competency level by earning a prescribed number of points. The student may also keep the quizzes and maps for later review and personal use.

The Map Activity Quizzes need not be done in any particular order, but teachers need to be aware that the quizzes vary in their level of difficulty. The point values for each quiz are shown in the right corner of each quiz, below the line for the student's name. The number of the quiz is on the top left corner of each quiz.

The Explorer Series of articles can be read to the classes or duplicated for the students'

use. Each has a Map Activity Quiz that pertains to the explorer discussed. The article and quiz may be given to a student at the same time for his or her study.

When a student has completed the requirements and obtained the total number of points necessary for a certificate, the student's name and the school organization should be printed or typed on the certificate, then signed and dated by the instructor in charge of the program.

There are four levels of awards. The points gained for each are cumulative. The highest award is the Explorer Certificate of Map Skill Proficiency.

Award	Requirements
Tourist	25 points
Traveler	50 points
Navigator	75 points
Explorer	100 points

To receive the Explorer Certificate of Map Skill Proficiency, a student must read all the Explorer Series articles and successfully complete all Explorer quizzes.

Students may want to make notebooks or booklets of the information the teacher gives them from the Lesson Plans, the Explorer Series, their work in the Map Activity Quizzes, the Appendix Maps, and their Certificates of Map Skill Proficiency. Duplicate Appendix Map 3, a book cover, for use as a front and back cover for such collections. This illustration is the title page of the first sea atlas in English, *The Mariner's Mirror*.

The MAP CORNER

MAPS: Their Makers and Users

Miguel de Cervantes

Journey over all the universe in a map, without the expense and fatigue of traveling, without suffering the inconveniences of heat, cold, hunger, and thirst.

Miguel de Cervantes

A map or chart laid upon a table sets men and women to dreaming. *What lies over that mountain range? Are there really people there? What will we find? Who will we find? Should we journey only in our fantasy?*

What better way to make a fanciful trip than with a map or a chart. Far-off countries and islands have captured the minds of men and women since they sat around campfires wondering and dreaming of what lay beyond a ridge, a hill, or expanse of water. A spot on the ground was made smooth with the palm of a hand. A stick was stuck in the dirt. *Here is where we are now.* Then, with a flourish, a line was drawn across the ground. *Here is where we will go.* The map was created!

The oldest known map was made on a clay tablet in Babylonia around 2300 B.C. Pressed into the wet clay by means of a stylus and then allowed to dry were the outlines of an estate lying in a valley surrounded by mountains. One can only wonder what went through the mind of the mapmaker or owner of the estate about what lay beyond the mountains.

The word *mappa* is a Latin derivative meaning cloth. Maps represent all or parts of the earth's surface. The word *charta,* also a Latin derivative, means paper. Charta or chart more specifically refers to a map of the sea or ocean. The sailors' chart became known as the *portolano* or the *portolan chart.*

By the fourteenth and fifteenth centuries portolans had been created to represent the Mediterranean and Black Seas and some of the Atlantic coast of Europe. They were mostly drawn on sheepskin. A system of lines of compass directions oriented to magnetic north made these charts particularly valuable to the mariners of that time. The charts linked recognizable landmarks on the coastline so that sailors could sail from one point to another. Only the coastline was shown with any accuracy or detail on the portolan since it was used exclusively by mariners.

Down through the centuries people have used various materials on which to represent their conception of the earth. They have used such materials as driftwood, boards, metal, stones, bones, palm leaves, shells, skins, leather, fabric, sand, and snow. Eskimos scratched maps on wood and ivory. In other cultures, more exotic materials have been

1

used; maps have even been woven into the designs of carpets and tapestries, or placed in tile work as mosaics.

The native inhabitants of the Marshall Islands in the Pacific used a unique system of stick charts. Using palm leaves tied together with fibers from plants, they devised a type of chart that allowed them to gauge the waves and currents on which they took their boats. Islands were marked on these charts by cowry shells and pieces of coral.

In China, during the Han Dynasty from 200 B.C. to 220 A.D., map making was very advanced. The evidence indicates that Chinese cartography reached a higher level of development than in any other nation of the world. Silk maps have recently been found that date back to the second century B.C. Rectangular grids were also superimposed on Chinese maps during these years. In later dynasties, maps were made that showed the drainage flow to China's coastline, settlements and rivers, and the Great Wall.

In 105 A.D., Ts'ai Lun made pulp from rag fibers and other materials and produced the first good writing paper. This material also became widely used in map making.

About 300 years before the birth of Christ, the Greeks made maps that depicted what they knew about the earth and the people who lived on it. The Greeks were the first to understand that the earth is a sphere. As a result of this knowledge they were able to develop the first projection, that is, a systematic representation of the earth drawn on a flat surface, or a map. Consequently, they also gave us the system of latitude and longitude.

Some of the most outstanding accomplishments of Greek science were the work of Eratosthenes. In the year 240 B.C. he was appointed head of the Library of Alexandria in Egypt. Because the Greeks accepted the idea that the earth was a sphere, it was logical that someone would attempt to determine the earth's circumference. While Eratosthenes was not the first to do this, his estimate was remarkably accurate, coming within 140 miles of the earth's meridional circumference of 24,860 miles.

Claudius Ptolemy

In what is now Italy, the Romans used maps for taxing purposes and for military ventures. As a result, they became excellent surveyors and created the forerunners of the road maps we use today.

Around 150 A.D., Claudius Ptolemy, at the Library of Alexandria in Egypt, created a guide to making maps that is known as the *Geographia*. This guide included instructions for making map and globe projections and a table of geographic coordinates of 8,000 localities, with their latitudes and longitudes. There was now a framework for fitting in new discoveries as they were made.

Ptolemy also calculated the circumference of the earth, as did Eratosthenes, but Ptolemy was in error since he determined the earth's circumference to be 18,000 miles. This figure was accepted throughout the Middle Ages and lead Columbus to believe that he had reached Asia when, in reality, he had discovered a new world, America.

Gerhard Kremer used the Latinized name of *Gerhardus Mercator*. This Flemish geographer and map maker created a projection of the world that bears his name (the Mercator projection) and was of great value to naviga-

2

tors. Mercator's map, if not properly understood, can lead to a mistaken perception of the relative sizes of land masses. For example, Greenland is shown as being larger than South America, when actually it is one-eighth as large (see Appendix Map 33). Mercator popularized the term *atlas* for a book of maps, although a French engraver, Laffery, drew the figure of the mythical Atlas carrying the world on his shoulders. He used the drawing on the title pages of his collections of maps.

Galileo Galilei (1564–1642) was an astronomer, the founder of modern physics, and a map maker. Galileo, who is usually known by his first name only, was the first astronomer to use the telescope. He constructed his own telescopes and used them for research. Through his discovery of the four satellites of the planet Jupiter, Galileo was able to prove visually Copernicus' theory that the earth moves on its axis. Galileo made some of the first lunar charts showing mountains, valleys, and craters.

As Europeans began to settle on the American continent and the colonies came into existence, a great need developed for mapping the land. Most maps of America, however, were

Galileo Galilei

made in Europe and bore European representations and symbols.

George Washington and Thomas Jefferson, who were both surveyors, had a great interest in mapping and conducting geographic

Gerhard Kremer (Gerhardus Mercator)

George Washington

3

Benjamin Franklin

Meriwether Lewis and William Clark

exploration in the colonies. Washington became acutely aware of the need for good maps when he lead the colonials' fight in the Revolutionary War.

In 1775, Benjamin Franklin, whose inventions and interests were of wide scope, made a chart of the limits of the Gulf Stream that was based on Fahrenheit thermometer readings.

As President of the United States, Thomas Jefferson wanted the Northwest to be explored. In 1801, plans were made to find a passageway through the Louisiana Territory (bought from France in 1803) and what was then known as the Oregon region. President Jefferson chose an Army captain, Meriwether Lewis, to head the expedition. Lewis selected a friend and former Army officer, William Clark, as second in command. Unofficially, they decided to split the command position between them, and have Clark serve as cartographer for the group.

Sacajawea, a Shoshone Indian woman, helped make possible the success of the Lewis and Clark expedition. Although not a principal guide for the expedition, she had an ability for finding food in the wilderness that could be used to supplement the staples the explorers had brought. When a boat overturned, her quick actions saved valuable articles needed by the expedition, and she won the confidence of an Indian tribe that presented a serious threat to the explorers.

4   Thomas Jefferson

Sacajawea served as a guide to Clark when the group split up on the return trip in 1806. She helped Clark through the mountain passes of the Continental Divide. Toussaint Charbonnea, her husband, served as an interpreter for Lewis and Clark. In 1805, when the couple joined the expedition along the Missouri River, in what was later to become North Dakota, Sacajawea was just 18 and a new mother. She carried her son with her on the trip.

Lewis and Clark were first guided by an English map of North America made by Arron Arrowsmith; later, they made their own maps. As the western part of America was explored and settled, much cartographic information was collected and very detailed maps of the United States were developed. By 1879, when the United States Geological Survey was begun, large-scale, detailed maps were available.

Excellent maps made it possible for women such as Annie S. Peck (1850–1935), an explorer and scholar, to take up mountain climbing. Ms. Peck graduated from the University of Michigan in 1878. She studied music in Germany and archaeology in Greece, and became a professor of Latin. When she was 45 she took up mountain climbing. She climbed the Matterhorn and other Alpine mountains in 1895. In 1904, she went to South America and climbed Mt. Sorata (20,500 feet) in Bolivia. Four years later she climbed Huascarán (21,812 feet) in Peru.

During the 1900s many roads crisscrossed America. The automobile gave Americans the freedom to travel in unprecedented numbers.

Sacajawea

The growing need for road maps was met by the oil companies, which provided maps to the gasoline stations. Organizations like the American Automobile Association were created to meet the traveler's primary need, and that need was for maps.

Then Americans took to the skies. Commercial and military travel called for a vast new technology in map making. Now maps are made for space travel and to explore the depths of the sea, fulfilling the prophetic words of Cervantes, "Journey over all the universe in a map."

5

Things to do with Maps

1. Cut out all the maps from the local newspaper for one week and arrange them on a bulletin board by city, county, or state, or by national or international place of origin.

2. Mark on an appropriate Appendix Map where stories in the daily newspaper originate.

3. Mark on a map where the news stories in news magazines originate.

4. Place North, South, East, and West signs in conspicuous places on the classroom walls.

5. Draw a map of the school building and yard and place a Compass Rose in the correct position on the map.

6. Cut out small local maps from advertisements in the newspaper and place them correctly on a larger city or county map.

7. Mark on a county or city map where stores are located whose addresses are in the newspaper.

8. Determine in which direction you live from a store that is advertised in a newspaper.

9. Mark on a map of your state where your two U. S. senators live.

10. Mark on a U. S. map where friends and relatives live.

11. Look at the weather report in the newspaper for the five cities with the highest and lowest temperatures in the United States and place the names in the correct areas on Appendix Map 5.

12. Place the names of the cities and towns discussed in the first section of your newspaper on Appendix Maps 33, 34, or 35.

13. Place the names of the birthplaces of the United States presidents on Appendix Map 5. Write the names of the presidents underneath.

14. Mark the location of the cities of the pro football franchises and the leagues to which they belong on Appendix Map 4. Mark the name of the team and the city. (Optional: Do the same for your favorite baseball, basketball, or hockey team.)

15. On Appendix Map 4 or 5, mark where your favorite college football teams are located.

16. Take notes on the news presented in a national network news program. List the places around the world that are discussed and mark those places on the appropriate national and world appendix maps.

17. Locate the state and national parks that are in your region on one of the regional appendix maps. Check an encyclopedia, atlas, or other reference aid to find where they are.

18. Browse through back issues of the *National Geographic.* Pick out the main or most interesting articles, find and mark the locations on appropriate Appendix Maps.

19. Choose a city in the United States to which you would like to travel. Mark a direct flight on the map from where you live. Which states would you fly over? Use Appendix Map 5. Would you cross a time zone? What time do you think you would arrive there if you left your town at 12 o'clock noon?

20. Write the name and location on Appendix Map 5 of the capitals of each state.

21. Trace the flow of the Gulf Stream on Appendix Map 33.

22. Write the names of the countries on Appendix Map 47 that border the Mediterranean Sea.

23. While some authorities differ, the following rivers are considered the longest in the world. Find them in an atlas and draw and label them on Appendix Map 33, 34, or 35.

River	Outflow	Length (miles)
Nile	Mediterranean	4,145
Amazon	Atlantic Ocean	4,000
Chang Jiang	East China Sea	3,964
Huang He	Yellow	2,903
Congo	Atlantic Ocean	2,900
Amur	Tatar Strait	2,744
Lena *Siberia*	Laptev Sea *Arctic*	2,734
Mackenzie	Arctic Ocean	2,635
Mekong *Twiland Laos*	South China Sea	2,600
Yenisey	Kara Sea	2,543
Missouri	Mississippi	2,533
Mississippi	Gulf of Mexico	2,348

24. The mountains listed below are the highest on their continents. Find them in an atlas and then mark their positions on Appendix Map 33, 34, or 35. Then check encyclopedias and atlases for other high mountains and mark their positions.

Continent	Mountain	Height (feet)
Asia	Mount Everest, China-Nepal	29,028
South America	Mount Aconcagua, Argentina	22,834
North America	Mount McKinley, Alaska	20,320
Africa	Kilimanjaro, Tanzania	19,340

25. Make a scrapbook of different maps found in the daily newspaper and news magazines over a two-week period. Divide the scrapbook by country and paste the maps in the correct categories.

26. Collect maps from the daily newspaper and news magazines for a two-week period. Classify them on a bulletin board in the following categories:

politics   products
population   religion
weather   hemisphere

Form other categories as appropriate.

27. Choose an appendix map for a country you are studying or one in which you are interested. Study about the country and do the following:

Locate and label the largest cities.
Locate and label places of interest.
Label places of historic significance.
Illustrate the sources of principal products.
Locate and label principal transportation centers.
Locate and label chief ports, if appropriate.
Draw the country's major rivers.
Draw the country's largest lakes.
Draw and label the states or provinces.

28. Draw the railroad lines or bus routes on Appendix Map 4 or a regional outline map.

29. Read the daily and Sunday comic pages and look for clues as to where the strip takes place. Write the name of the strip on an appropriate appendix map.

30. List the top ten television programs watched by the class. Mark on an appropriate appendix map where the geographic setting is for each show.

31. On an appropriate regional, national, or world appendix map, label the cities listed in the newspaper weather report and give their high and low temperatures.

32. On appropriate appendix maps, mark where the major battles were fought during a war the class may be studying.

33. As a class activity, list the 10 or 20 greatest humans who ever lived (parents may advise in this activity) and then mark their birthplaces and their spheres of influence during their lifetimes on an appropriate appendix map.

34. Peter Jenkins, a young man discouraged about his country, decided a few years ago to walk across the United States to find the real America. Trace his route on the appropriate appendix maps. Information about his travels and maps tracing his route can be found in the *National Geographic,* April 1977, vol. 151, no. 4; and August 1979, vol. 156, no. 2; and in Jenkins' books, *A Walk Across America,* 1979, and *The Walk West: A Walk Across America 2,* 1981 (William Morrow & Company, Inc.).

35. Ask the school librarian to discuss the travel section found in the school library. Create map activities from these books.

Map Corner Lesson Plans

Lesson Plan for Geographic Terms

Lesson No.: _One_

Grade: _5_

Name: _Brad_

Date: _5/1/14_

Objectives

1. To define geographic terms.
2. To identify geographic concepts on maps.
3. _To define geographic terms_
4. _To identify geographic concepts on maps_

Materials, Resources, and Equipment

Atlas _Yes_

Appendix maps _Yes_

Classroom maps _Yes_

Encyclopedias _Yes_

Textbooks _Yes_

Procedures

The word *geography* comes from the Greek *geōgraphia.* The *gē* means earth. *Graphē* means description. From this is derived the suffix *graphy,* meaning writing. Geography is the description, through various written forms, of the earth. Geographic terms are important for helping students develop accuracy in their descriptions and in making themselves clearly understood.

The geographic terms in the sets that follow can be better understood if students first learn the skills necessary for using the reference aids listed under the Materials, Resources, and Equipment list of this lesson plan. The terms are alphabetically listed in eight sets of three definitions each. Duplicate these sets and give them to the students for small-group or individual study and instruction. Students are to learn the definitions and then locate examples on maps or find illustrations in textbooks.

On the back of each set, students can write the name of their source and page numbers for documentation purposes. When all eight sets are completed, the students can cut out a back and front cover from construction paper. The entire set is then stapled together on the left-hand side. These booklets are useful for future review.

continued on next page

Evaluation Activities

Include a number of different evaluation activities here that are applicable to your class. For example:

1. Make a test that requires matching geographic terms with their definitions.
2. Mark the locations of specific geographic terms on appropriate appendix maps.

14

Geographic Terms—Set I

1. **bay**—a body of water partially closed off by land with a wide opening to the sea.
   Locate
   Hudson Bay   San Francisco Bay

2. **butte**—a small mesa—a hill or mountain that rises very abruptly above an area—the top is flat and the side slopes steeply.
   Locate
   Butte, Montana
   Buttes in the western part of the United States—find an illustration.

3. **canyon**—a narrow chasm or valley with steep sides or cliff walls formed by the erosion of running water—*synonym:* **gorge.**
   Locate
   Arizona's Grand Canyon

Geographic Terms—Set II

1. **cape**—land, smaller than a peninsula, that projects into a sea, lake, or ocean from a coastline.
   Locate
   "heel" and "toe" of Italy   Cape Canaveral, Florida

2. **coastline**—the place where land and water meet along the shoreline —often determines the shape of a country or state.
   Locate
   Eastern and western seaboards of the United States
   Coastlines of the Great Lakes

3. **continent**—one of seven main land masses on the earth's surface.
   Locate
   Africa   Europe
   Antarctica   North America
   Asia   South America
   Australia

The Map Corner

Geographic Terms—Set III

1. **delta**—a deposit of mud and sand at the mouth of a river, often triangular in shape.
   Locate
   Mississippi delta   Nile delta

2. **fjord**—a long, narrow, deep sea inlet between steep cliffs.
   Locate
   Norway   Alaska

3. **gulf**—a large body of water extending from an ocean or sea into an area partially enclosed by land—a bay is much smaller than a gulf.
   Locate
   Gulf of Mexico   Gulf of Alaska
   Gulf of California

Geographic Terms—Set IV

1. **harbor**—a protected anchorage deep enough to shelter ships—
   synonym: **port**
   Locate
   Rio de Janiero   New York

2. **island**—a body of land completely surrounded by water (a sea, river, or lake)—an island is smaller than a continent.
   Locate
   Puerto Rico   Skye, Scotland

2. **isthmus**—a narrow strip of land connecting two larger bodies of land.
   Locate
   Isthmus of Panama   Isthmus of Kar, Thailand

16

Geographic Terms—Set V

1. **lake**—a large body of salt or fresh water with land surrounding it.
   Locate
   The Great Lakes   Lake Okeechobee, Florida
   The Great Salt Lake, Utah

2. **lowland**—land that is low compared to the surrounding area or that rises only slightly above the level of the water.
   Locate
   Land along the Mississippi River
   Florida
   South Carolina

3. **mesa**—a flat-topped hill with sides descending steeply to the land surrounding it—a **butte** is a small mesa.
   Locate
   Southwestern United States

Geographic Terms—Set VI

1. **mountain**—a large piece of land rising higher than a hill and generally having steep sides.
   Locate
   The Rocky Mountains   The Swiss Alps
   The Appalachian Mountains

2. **ocean**—the body of salt water that covers 72 percent of the surface of the earth.
   Locate
   Atlantic Ocean   Indian Ocean
   Pacific Ocean   Arctic Ocean

3. **peninsula**—a projection of land nearly surrounded by water.
   Locate
   Italian Peninsula   Scandanavian Peninsula
   Danish Peninsula

The Map Corner

Geographic Terms—Set VII

1. **plain**—land without hills or mountains, almost level, and generally grassy with few trees.
   Locate
   Plains of North America and find an illustration
   Plains in Europe

2. **plateau**—raised or elevated piece of land that is broad and flat—*synonym:* **tableland.**
   Locate
   Iran   Tibet

3. **river**—a long, narrow stream of water that empties into a lake, ocean, or other body of water.
   Locate
   Mississippi River   Nile River
   Amazon River

Geographic Terms—Set VIII

1. **sea**—a large body of water enclosed to some degree by land.
   Locate
   Mediterranean Sea   Red Sea
   North Sea

2. **strait**—a narrow body of water connecting two larger bodies of water.
   Locate
   Strait of Bosporus   Hudson Strait
   Strait of Gibralter   Davis Strait

3. **valley**—a long, low depression between ranges of hills or mountains.
   Locate
   Death Valley   Tigris-Euphrates Valley
   Rhine Valley   Nile Valley

18

Lesson Plan for Road Map Use

Lesson No.: _____   Name: _____

Grade: _____   Date: _____

Objectives

1. To determine driving distance from one place to another.
2. To develop interest in places to visit.

3. _____

4. _____

Materials, Resources, and Equipment

Appendix Maps 4 and 5
Appendix Map of your region of
   the country
Atlas
Encyclopedia

Road maps
Travel brochures
Tour books
Travel magazines

Procedures

Toward the end of the 1970s, people in the United States were driving 1,520,000,000,000 miles a year: That's 1.52 trillion miles in a year's time! With all this travel, students have many opportunities to learn how to use maps. Here are some activities to try in the classroom.

1. Have students bring to class road maps, travel brochures, used "triptiks" and tour books from the American Automobile Association, and other travel and map information materials from automobile associations. Use these for map skill lessons.
2. Teach students how to use the mileage tables from road maps. Find the distance from:

Cleveland, Ohio to Chicago, Illinois
Detroit, Michigan to Denver, Colorado
Louisville, Kentucky to Los Angeles, California
Omaha, Nebraska to Philadelphia, Pennsylvania
Seattle, Washington to Miami, Florida.

_____ to _____

_____ to _____

_____ to _____

_____ to _____

continued on next page

19

3. Mark and label the cities listed above on Appendix Map 5.
4. List the states a person would travel through while making the above trips.
5. Study travel brochures, tour books, encyclopedias, travel magazines, and other related materials for vacation places. Choose a vacation spot and trace the best routes to get there on a road map. Then mark the routes on Appendix Map 5. Have the students do this individually or in small groups.
6. Make a list of the safe driving tips found in the reference materials. Have the students take the list home for discussion with their families, particularly before a trip or vacation period.
7. Find the Blue Ridge Parkway on a road map. Trace the route on Appendix Map 4.
8. Use an atlas to find the major highways in the United States. Trace and list the routes and route numbers on Appendix Map 5.
9. Use an atlas to find the major national parks in the United States. Outline them on Appendix Map 4 and label them by name.
10. Have the students discuss with their parents where out-of-town relatives and close friends live. They should list on a sheet of paper their names and the cities and states in which they live. Have them bring the list to school and mark the information on Appendix Map 5. Use any available reference materials to help determine where relatives and friends live. Determine who lives the farthest away but still inside the United States. What route(s) would students take to visit relatives and friends? What states would they pass through?

Evaluation Activities

Include a number of different evaluation activities that are applicable to your class. For example:
1. List five places you have never been to and explain why you would want to go there.
2. Determine how far from home the above places are and explain how the mileage was determined.

Lesson Plan for Thunderstorms

Lesson No.: _____ Name: _____

Grade: _____ Date: _____

Objectives

1. To learn the safety rules that should be observed during a thunderstorm.
2. To learn what can be done to prevent personal harm during thunderstorms.
3. To develop an understanding of the serious effects of lightning, thunder, tornadoes, flash flooding, and hail.
4. To chart on a map the widespread destruction caused by thunderstorms during one summer month.

Materials, Resources, and Equipment

Appendix Map 5
Appendix Map of your region
  of the country
A Month of Storms

Thunderstorm Safety Rules
Thunderstorm Effects: Lightning,
  Thunder, Tornadoes, Flash
  Flooding, and Hail

Procedures

At any given moment, nearly 2,000 thunderstorms are occurring over the earth's surface. The frequency and potential violence of thunderstorms make them one of nature's worst killers and destroyers. Students need to become aware of the havoc thunderstorms can cause and how they can protect themselves.

"A Month of Storms" tells of the destruction that thunderstorms did in various parts of the country during one average summer month. Mark and illustrate on Appendix Map 5 where these storms took place.

Assign students to listen to television and radio weather reports and mark on Appendix Map 5 and on the appendix map for the region in which they reside where thunderstorm activity has occurred. Students should bring their maps to class for comparison and discussion. Other weather conditions may also be noted.

continued on next page

THUNDERSTORM SAFETY RULES

If you plan to be outdoors, check the latest weather forecast and keep a weather eye on the sky. At signs of an impending storm—towering thunderheads, darkening skies, lightning, increasing winds—tune in your radio or television for the latest weather information.

When a thunderstorm threatens, get inside a home, a large building, or an all-metal (not convertible) automobile. Do not use the telephone except for emergencies.

If you are caught outside, do not stand underneath a natural lightning rod, such as a tall isolated tree or a telephone pole. Avoid projecting above the surrounding landscape, for example, by standing on a hilltop. In a forest, seek shelter in a low area under a thick growth of small trees. In open areas, go to a low place such as a ravine or valley.

Get off or away from open water, tractors, and other metal farm equipment, or small metal vehicles such as motorcycles, bicycles, or golf carts. Stay away from wire fences, clotheslines, metal pipes, and rails. Put down golf clubs. If you are in a group in the open, spread out and keep several yards apart.

If you are caught out in a level field or prairie far from shelter, and if you feel your hair stand on end, lightning may be about to strike you. Drop to your knees and bend forward putting your hands on your knees. Do not lie flat on the ground.

Persons struck by lightning receive a severe electrical shock and may be burned, but they carry no electrical charge and can be handled safely. Even someone "killed" by lightning can be revived by prompt action. When a group has been struck, the apparently dead should be treated first.

The American National Red Cross says that if a victim is not breathing, first aid should be rendered within four to six minutes to prevent irrevocable damage to the brain. Give mouth-to-mouth resuscitation once every five seconds to adults and once every three seconds to infants and small children, until medical help arrives.

If the victim is not breathing and has no pulse, cardiopulmonary resuscitation—a combination of mouth-to-mouth resuscitation and external cardiac compression—is necessary. This treatment should be administered only by persons with proper training.

Victims who appear to be only stunned or otherwise unhurt may also need attention. Check for burns, especially at fingers and toes, and next to buckles and jewelry.

A MONTH OF STORMS

Tucson, Arizona experienced its most violent thunderstorm in over a decade. Wind gusts up to 67 miles per hour and heavy rains caused damage of $52 million. Ten airplanes were severely damaged. Several dozen houses lost their roofs, and streets were flooded with water two or three feet deep.

Two tornadoes passed through the city of Canton, Illinois, killing 2, injuring 69, destroying about 100 homes and 50 mobile homes, and damaging 127 downtown businesses.

Three days of thunderstorms dropped five to eight inches of rain over most of New Jersey. Flash floods caused five drownings. Damage to crops and property was $30 million.

Thunderstorm winds of 60 miles per hour churned up high waves at Codorus State Park, Pennsylvania, causing $500,000 damage to boats and docks.

Three inches of rain fell in Las Vegas, Nevada, causing flash floods that destroyed or damaged 700 vehicles, with losses of $3½ million in damages in the northern part of the city.

In Tampa, Florida, a 16-year old boy was killed by lightning while walking along a railroad track. An Iowa woman was struck when she ran outside to close her car windows.

A 15-minute barrage of hail destroyed a 43-acre orchard crop in Washington State. In western New York, lightning that struck a large tree killed one person and injured 12 others who had taken refuge there.

In North Carolina, lightning killed one woman and injured two other persons in a group that was having a fish fry under a metal-roofed carport.

In a Mississippi lighthouse, a 12-year-old girl was killed and eight others injured when lightning struck. The young girl was leaning against a steel support.

Strong thunderstorm winds on Delaware Bay capsized a 34-foot houseboat. Two occupants drowned.

In Oklahoma two people were injured when strong thunderstorm winds destroyed three mobile homes—not tied down.

Two people boating on a Michigan lake were injured when lightning struck the mast of their sailboat.

Thunderstorm Effects
Lightning, Thunder, Tornadoes, Flash Flooding, and Hail

Lightning

Man has long marveled at lightning. It was the ultimate weapon of the gods of ancient civilization. Today, lightning is subjected to scientific scrutiny, but it is no less awesome, and it still deserves respect.

National Center for Health Statistics data for recent years show that lightning kills about 125 Americans per year and injures more than 500. Property loss is estimated in the hundreds of millions of dollars annually.

Lightning is an effect of electrification within a thunderstorm. As the thunderstorm develops, interactions of charged particles produce an intense electrical field within the cloud. A large positive charge is usually concentrated in the frozen upper layers of the cloud, and a large negative charge along with a smaller positive area is found in the lower portions.

The earth is normally negatively charged with respect to the atmosphere. But as the thunderstorm passes over the ground, the negative charge in the base of the cloud induces a positive charge on the ground below and for several miles around the storm. The ground charge follows the storm like an electrical shadow, growing stronger as the negative cloud charge increases. The attraction between positive and negative charges makes the positive ground current flow up buildings, trees, and other elevated objects in an effort to establish a flow of current. But air, which is a poor conductor of electricity, insulates the cloud and ground charges, preventing a flow of current until huge electrical charges are built up.

Lightning occurs when the difference between the positive and negative charges—the electrical potential—becomes great enough to overcome the resistance of the insulating air, and to force a conductive path for current to flow between the two charges. Potential in these cases can be as much as 100 million volts. Lightning strokes proceed from cloud to cloud, cloud to ground, or, where high structures are involved, from ground to cloud.

Thunder

Thunder is the sound produced by explosive expansion of air heated by a lightning stroke. When lightning is close by, the thunder sounds like a sharp crack. More distant strokes produce growling and rumbling noises, a result of the sound being refracted and modified by the turbulent environment of a thunderstorm. Because the speed of light is about a million times that of sound, we see a lightning bolt before the sound of the thunder reaches us. This makes it possible to estimate the distance (in miles) to a lightning stroke by counting the number of seconds between lightning and thunder and dividing by five.

Tornadoes

The most destructive child of a thunderstorm is the tornado, a violently rotating column of air which descends from a thunderstorm cloud system. Tornadoes move at about 30

continued on next page

24

Thunderstorm Effects, *continued*

miles per hour; however, some move very slowly, while others speed along at 60 miles per hour or more. The average path of a tornado is about a quarter of a mile wide and a few miles long. But some have cut a swath a mile wide and 300 miles long. The destructive winds of a tornado can exceed 200 miles per hour.

In an average year, tornadoes in the United States claim about 100 lives and cause hundreds of millions of dollars' damage.

Flash Flooding

Flash floods can result from heavy rains associated with thunderstorms. Rainfall of over four inches in a few hours is recorded many times each year. In the U.S. the record rainfall for one hour exceeds 10 inches.

On June 9, 1972, stationary thunderstorms over the Black Hills of South Dakota resulted in flash floods that took the lives of over 230 people in and near Rapid City.

In 1970, 11 inches of rain in less than 24 hours produced a spectacular and terrifying flash flood in Arizona. The rates at which streams rose were described by many as unbelievable. Uprooted trees, huge boulders, fences, automobiles, and small buildings were swept downstream; 23 lives were lost.

In recent years, flash floods have taken an average of more than 100 lives a year and have been reported in almost every state.

Hail

Hailstones are precipitation in the form of lumps of ice that occur during some thunderstorms. Hailstones range from pea size to the size of a grapefruit. They're usually round, but may also be conical, or irregular in shape, some with pointed projections.

Hail is most devastating to crops. Losses in 1973, for example, were $585 million for the 18 hardest-hit states and $680 million for the United States as a whole. In addition, there was $68 million damage to property.

Evaluation Activities

Include a number of different evaluation activities that are applicable to your class. For example:

1. Have a small group discuss the rules of safety to follow during a thunderstorm. At the end of the discussion ask the students to list the points that were made and those that were overlooked.
2. After studying "A Month of Storms," mark on the appropriate appendix map where the storms occurred.

Lesson Plan for Tracking Hurricanes

Lesson No.: _____   Name: _____

Grade: _____   Date: _____

Objectives

1. To learn how to keep oneself safe during a hurricane.
2. To understand the nature of a hurricane.
3. To learn how to track a hurricane by latitude and longitude.

Materials, Resources, and Equipment

Appendix Map 25 or 26   Hurricane Tracking Table
Hurricanes   Terms to Know
Hurricane Safety Rules   General reference map
How to Track a Hurricane   Globe

Procedures

The information that follows can be duplicated for classroom study. When a hurricane spawns in the Atlantic, students can track its progress by listening to radio and television broadcasts to learn its latitude and longitude as well as other pertinent information. After noting the information on the Hurricane Tracking Table, they can determine its position on a general reference map or globe and mark the position on Appendix Map 25 or 26.

Evaluation Activities

Include a number of different evaluation activities that are applicable to your class. For example:
1. Ask each student to write a letter to a parent or relative describing what he or she believes are the five most important rules to follow in the event of a hurricane.
2. Write on the chalkboard a number of longitude and latitude coordinates typical of a hurricane's path, and ask the students to trace the path on an appropriate appendix map.

Hurricane Safety Rules

Hurricane advisories will help you save your life . . . but you must help.
Follow these safety rules during hurricane emergencies:

1. **Enter each hurricane season prepared.** Every June through November, recheck your supply of boards, tools, batteries, nonperishable foods, and the other equipment you will need when a hurricane strikes your town.

2. **When you hear the first tropical cyclone advisory,** listen for future messages; this will prepare you for a hurricane emergency well in advance of the issuance of watches and warnings.

3. **When your area is covered by a hurricane watch,** continue normal activities, but stay tuned to radio or television for all National Weather Service advisories. Remember, a hurricane watch means possible danger within 24 hours; if the danger materializes, a hurricane warning will be issued. Meanwhile, keep alert. Ignore rumors.

4. **When your area receives a hurricane warning: Plan your time** before the storm arrives and avoid the last-minute hurry which might leave you marooned, or unprepared.
   Keep calm until the emergency has ended.
   Leave low-lying areas that may be swept by high tides or storm waves.
   Leave mobile homes for more substantial shelter. They are particularly vulnerable to overturning during strong winds. Damage can be minimized by securing mobile homes with heavy cables anchored in concrete footing.
   Moor your boat securely before the storm arrives, or evacuate it to a designated safe area. When your boat is moored, leave it, and don't return once the wind and waves are up.
   Board up windows or protect them with storm shutters or tape. Danger to small windows is mainly from wind-driven debris. Larger windows may be broken by wind pressure.
   Secure outdoor objects that might be blown away or uprooted. Garbage cans, garden tools, toys, signs, porch furniture, and a number of other harmless items become missiles of destruction in hurricane winds. Anchor them or store them inside before the storm strikes.
   Store drinking water in clean bathtubs, jugs, bottles, and cooking utensils; your town's water supply may be contaminated by flooding or damaged by hurricane floods.
   Check your battery-powered equipment. Your radio may be your only link with the world outside the hurricane, and emergency cooking facilities, lights, and flashlights will be essential if utilities are interrupted.
   Keep your car fueled. Service stations may be inoperable for several days after the storm strikes, due to flooding or interrupted electrical power.

Beware the Eye of the Hurricane
If the calm storm center passes directly overhead, there will be a lull in the wind lasting from a few minutes to half an hour or more. Stay in a safe place unless emergency repairs are absolutely necessary. But remember, at the other side of the eye, the winds rise very rapidly to hurricane force, and come from the opposite direction.

Stay at home, if it is sturdy and on high ground; if it is not, move to a designated shelter, and stay there until the storm is over.
Remain indoors during the hurricane. Travel is extremely dangerous when

continued on next page

Hurricane Safety Rules, *continued*

winds and tides are whipping through your area.

Monitor the storm's position through National Weather Service advisories.

5. **When the hurricane has passed:**
Seek necessary medical care at Red Cross disaster stations or hospitals.
Stay out of disaster areas. Unless you are qualified to help, your presence might hamper first-aid and rescue work.
Drive carefully along debris-filled streets. Roads may be undermined and may collapse under the weight of a car. Slides along cuts are also a hazard.
Avoid loose or dangling wires, and report them immediately to your power company or the nearest law enforcement officer.
Report broken sewer or water mains to the water department.

Prevent fires. Lowered water pressure may make fire fighting difficult.
Check refrigerated food for spoilage if power has been off during the storm.

Remember that hurricanes moving inland can cause severe flooding. Stay away from river banks and streams.

Tornadoes spawned by hurricanes are among the storms' worst killers. When a hurricane approaches, listen for tornado watches and warnings. A tornado watch means tornadoes are expected to develop. A tornado warning means a tornado has actually been sighted. When your area receives a tornado warning, seek inside shelter immediately, preferably below ground level. If a tornado catches you outside, move away from its path at a right angle. If there is no time to escape, lie flat in the nearest depression, such as a ditch or ravine.

Hurricane watches means a hurricane may threaten an area within 24 hours. Hurricane warnings mean a hurricane is expected to strike an area within 24 hours.

How to Track a Hurricane

Advisories are numbered consecutively for each storm, and describe the present and forecast position and intensity of the storm.* Tropical cyclone advisories are issued at six-hour intervals—at midnight, 6 a.m., noon, and 6 p.m., Eastern Daylight Time. Bulletins provide additional information. Each message gives the name, eye position, intensity, and forecast movement of the tropical cyclone.

Hurricane eye positions are given by

*Tropical cyclones are not given names until they reach the storm stage—that is, closed isobars, rotary circulation, and winds over 39 miles per hour (34 knots).

latitude (for example, 13.2 degrees North) and longitude (for example, 57.8 degrees West), to the nearest one-tenth of one degree. When the storm moves within range of the radar fence, eye position may also be given as statute miles and compass direction from a specified point.

When you receive a tropical cyclone advisory, note the advisory number, eye position, intensity, and forecast direction of movement in the table at right. Then mark the eye position on the tracking chart. Because hurricanes change direction very quickly, you should concentrate more on where the storm will go than where it has been.

Hurricane Tracking Table

Storm Name	Advisory Number	Position						Maximum Wind (mph)	Central Pressure (inches Hg.)	Forward Speed (mph)	Direction	Forecast			
												Movement		Intensity	
		Date	Time (EDT)	Latitude (°N)	Longitude (°W)	Miles	from					Forward Speed (mph)	Direction	Increasing	Decreasing

Terms to Know

By international agreement, *tropical cyclone* is the general term for all cyclonic circulations originating over tropical waters, classified by form and intensity as follows:

Tropical disturbance: rotary circulation slight or absent at surface but sometimes better developed aloft, no closed isobars (lines of equal atmospheric pressure) and no strong winds, a common phenomenon in the tropics.

Tropical depression: one or more closed isobars and some rotary circulation at surface, highest wind speed 39 miles per hour (34 knots).

Tropical storm: closed isobars, distinct rotary circulation, highest wind speed 39–73 miles per hour (34–63 knots).

Hurricane: closed isobars, strong and very pronounced rotary circulation, wind speed of 74 miles per hour (64 knots) or more.

Small-craft warning: When a hurricane moves within a few hundred miles of the coast, advisories warn small-craft operators to take precautions and not to venture into the open ocean.

Gale warning: When winds of 38–55 miles per hour (33–48 knots) are expected, a gale warning is added to the advisory message.

Storm warning: When winds of 55–74 miles per hour (48–64 knots) are expected, a storm warning is added to the advisory message. Gale and storm warnings indicate the coastal area to be affected by the warning, the time during which the warning will apply, and the expected intensity of the disturbance.

When gale or storm warnings are part of a tropical cyclone advisory, they may change to a hurricane warning if the storm continues along the coast.

Hurricane watch: If the hurricane continues its advance and threatens coastal and inland regions, a hurricane watch is added to the advisory, covering a specified area and duration. A hurricane watch means that hurricane conditions are a real possibility; it does *not* mean they are imminent. When a hurricane watch is issued, everyone in the area covered by the watch should listen for further advisories and be prepared to act quickly if hurricane warnings are issued.

Hurricane warning: When hurricane conditions are expected within 24 hours, a hurricane warning is added to the advisory. Hurricane warnings identify coastal areas where winds of at least 74 miles per hour are expected to occur. A warning may also describe coastal areas where dangerously high water or exceptionally high waves are forecast, even though winds may be less than hurricane force.

When the hurricane warning is issued, all precautions should be taken immediately. Hurricane warnings are seldom issued more than 24 hours in advance. If the hurricane's path is unusual or erratic, the warnings may be issued only a few hours before the beginning of hurricane conditions. Precautionary actions should begin as soon as a hurricane warning is announced.

Lesson Plan for Bird Migration Routes

Lesson No.: _____   Name: _____

Grade: _____   Date: _____

Objectives

1. To learn the migration routes of various birds in the Western Hemisphere.
2. To determine which birds migrate in the students' state and where each bird flies.

3. _____

4. _____

Materials, Resources, and Equipment

Appendix Map 29
Appendix Map 30
Atlas

Globe
National Geographic, August 1979, vol., 156, no. 2, pp. 154–193.

Procedures

Encyclopedias generally carry a great deal of information about birds: What they are, how to watch them, how they fly, their various nesting places, their colors, how they raise their young, their cooperation with animals, their intelligence, what they do for man, how to care for them, how to study them, wildlife refuges and sanctuaries, and of great interest, how they migrate.

Many birds fly nonstop from North America to South America. Not only can they travel 2,500 miles, but they fly about 4 miles high in the sky! The arctic tern flies from the top of the world to the bottom and back again, a distance of about 20,000 to 25,000 miles.

Scientists theorize that birds find their direction in a variety of ways. They may follow coastlines or rivers, they may use the sun or stars to determine their course, or they may feel the magnetic force of the earth and use it to help locate their destination.

Some birds fly at night, and some fly leisurely, stopping to rest every few hours. Some go ahead of their mates to select a nesting spot, others go together. They follow no set pattern other than to migrate every year.

continued on next page

Lesson Plan for Bird Migration Routes, *continued*

Here are some things to do to learn about birds and their migration habits:

1. Study about birds in an encyclopedia or any books your librarian may suggest. (See *National Geographic,* August 1979, vol., 156, no. 2, pp. 154–193. This issue contains a full-scale map of the Western Hemisphere and an illustrated Map of Bird Migrations in the Americas.)

2. Study Appendix Map 30 on Bird Migration Routes. Determine the route of one of your favorite birds. Trace this migratory route on Appendix Map 29 and then with your finger on the globe. Take note of the areas over which the bird flies.

3. List the countries which the bird you are studying flies over or comes near on its trip.

4. According to Appendix Map 30, which bird or birds fly south from your state? What states, countries, or bodies of water do they fly over? Where do they spend the winter?

Evaluation Activities

Include a number of different evaluation activities that are applicable to your class. For example:

1. On an appropriate appendix map trace the migration patterns of three birds that fly to Central or South America. Mark the names of the bodies of water and countries they fly over and where they fly to.

2. List three birds from the state in which you live and the country(ies) to which they fly.

Lesson Plan for Monarch Butterfly Migration

Lesson No.: _____ Name: _____

Grade: _____ Date: _____

Objectives

1. To find the migratory pattern of the Monarch butterfly on a map or globe.
2. To determine where Monarch butterflies congregate.

3. _____

4. _____

Materials, Resources, and Equipment

Appendix map 22   Encyclopedia
Atlas   *National Geographic,* August 1976,
Globe   vol., 150, no. 2, pp. 161–173.

Procedures

Monarch
Butterfly

Imagine a small butterfly, the Monarch, weighing only one fiftieth of an ounce, flying from the United States to the Sierra Madre Mountains just north of Mexico City, spending the winter there with millions of other Monarchs, and then returning to the United States—a round-trip of 4,000 miles!

These gallant, beautiful insects, with the latinized name of *Danaus plexippus,* have been making this yearly pilgrimage long before man ever came to the Northern Hemisphere. The Monarchs in the west spend their winters between Monterey and Los Angeles, California. However, their Mexican breeding area has been discovered only in the last few years (see *National Geographic,* August 1976, vol., 150, no. 2, pp. 161–173). Here, many Monarchs breed in an extremely small area; in fact, one scientist watched as a pine bough three inches thick broke under the weight of them!

The life cycle of the Monarch butterfly follows this sequence: A female deposits an egg on the underside of a milkweed leaf. The egg is extremely small, about the size of a pinhead. Anywhere from 3 to 12 days later, a striped caterpillar emerges and feeds voraciously on the milkweed plant. In fact, it increases its weight 2,700 times. (If an 8-pound baby did the same thing, it would weigh 216,000 pounds!) The Monarch then emerges. The entire process takes about five weeks.

continued on next page

36

Lesson Plan for Monarch Butterfly Migration, *continued*

These delicate creatures have an interesting way of protecting themselves from most birds. They eat from the poisonous milkweed plant. This poison, although it enters the butterflies' systems, does not damage them. However, when birds try to eat them, the birds contract a severe case of nausea. Understandably, birds find it much more convenient to look elsewhere for food.

Scientists have been putting adhesive stickers on the Monarch butterflies' wings for a number of years. These stickers have an address on them that a person should write to if he or she finds a Monarch butterfly. In this way more information can be gained as to their travel patterns.

Here are some things to do to learn more about Monarch butterflies:

1. Read in an encyclopedia and the *National Geographic* about Monarch butterflies (see the August, 1976 and April, 1963 issues). Trace the migration patterns on a globe or map in an atlas using Appendix Map 22 as a guide.
2. Study Appendix Map 22 and find out if Monarchs breed, concentrate, or winter in your area.
3. Determine what states have the greatest concentrations of Monarch butterflies.
4. Determine how long it would take a Monarch to return to your state from its Mexican breeding area if it flew 10 miles a day (or 30 miles a day). What states would it pass through?

Evaluation Activities

Include a number of different evaluation activities that are applicable to your class. For example:

1. Trace on an appropriate appendix map the route the Monarch butterfly travels if it lives in your state.
2. On Appendix Map 21 mark where the Monarch butterfly breeds during the winter.

Map Activity Quizzes

Map Activity Quiz 1: Scale

You will need:

Appendix Map 5
Atlas
Reference maps
Encyclopedia
Globe

Name: _____

Points: _____5_____

If you look up the word *scale* in the dictionary, you will find it has many meanings. In relation to maps, scale is a representation of distance. A one-inch line may mean one mile, 100 miles, or even 1,000 miles. The scale may also be set in the metric system of centimeters, meters, and kilometers.

Sometimes the scale is written as a fraction, $\frac{1}{62,500}$, or as a ratio, 1:62,500. This would mean that a one-inch line on a map would represent about one mile on earth or approximately 62,500 inches (exact scale 1" = 1 mile is 1:63,360).

1. Find four different maps of the United States in encyclopedias, atlases, road maps, reference maps, or Appendix Map 5. Using your ruler and the scales on these maps as guides, determine the approximate length of the following states in miles or kilometers:
   Florida (Pensacola to Jacksonville)
   Florida (Jacksonville to Miami)
   Tennessee (northern border)
   Texas (Amarillo to Brownsville)
   Pennsylvania (Philadelphia to Pittsburgh)
   Montana (northern border)
   The length and width of your state
2. Cut a string to represent the length of the scale on your globe. With the string determine the approximate widths in miles or kilometers of the following countries:
   United States   China
   Union of Soviet Socialist   Australia
         Republics   Canada
   Brazil   India

(Scales on maps of large areas of the earth, like hemispheric or world maps, are only correct for some parts of those maps. For measuring long distances on the earth, a globe is always better.)

41

Map Activity Quiz 2: Equator

Name: _____

You will need:

Points: _____5_____

    Appendix Map 33, or 34
    Globe
    Encyclopedia

    The earth has a North Pole and a South Pole. The equator is a line, equidistant from the North and South Poles, dividing the earth into equal halves. The equator is 24,903 miles around the earth or approximately 25,000 miles. The top half of the earth is the Northern Hemisphere; the lower half is the Southern Hemisphere. *Hemi* means half and *sphere* means ball: half a ball.

1. With a globe, trace your finger around the earth. Then hold the globe with your right hand on the Northern Hemisphere and your left hand on the Southern Hemisphere.
2. On a world appendix map, write the names of the oceans that the equator crosses or intersects. Check with your globe.
3. What major continents does the equator intersect? Label them on your map.
4. Two major rivers of the world are near or are intersected by the equator. What countries carry the major flow of these rivers?
5. Draw the approximate locations of these rivers on your map. Then look up the word *equator* in an encyclopedia and, in the spaces below, write two facts about it.

_____

_____

_____

_____

Map Activity Quiz 3: Latitude

You will need:

    Appendix Map 33, 34, or 35
    Globe

Name: _____

Points: ____5_____

    Parallels of latitude are imaginary lines running east and west around the earth. They are always an equal distance apart and, therefore, never meet. These parallels or lines measure *latitude*, which means width. Those parallels north of the equator are called lines of north latitude. Those south of the equator are called lines of south latitude. Latitude indicates distance north or south of the equator. The equator is at 0° (zero degrees), so the parallels north and south of the equator are used to measure latitudes or degrees north and south. From the equator to the North Pole is 90° and from the equator to the South Pole is 90°.

    Parallels of latitude are usually shown on maps and globes at 10°, 15°, or 30° intervals. For most of us, all that is needed to determine a line of latitude is to make an approximation between two specific lines already drawn on a map or globe.

1. On a globe find the equator, which circles the earth at its midpoint. From the equator trace your finger north (or south, if you live below the equator) until you come to your state or province. Approximately what parallel of latitude is nearest to your town or city? Write the degree of latitude in the space below.

2. What approximate parallels of latitude are the following cities located on: Miami, Florida; Boston, Massachusetts; London, England; Tokyo, Japan; Rio de Janiero, Brazil; Calcutta, India? Mark them and their lines of latitude on an appendix map.

3. Choose ten other cities in ten different countries of the world and mark them with their latitudes on your map.

_____

_____

_____

_____

The Map Corner

Meridians of longitude are imaginary lines running north and south around the earth. Because the meridians meet at the North and South Poles, they are not always equal distances apart. The meridians or longitude lines are drawn at intervals of 15° or 30° on most maps. The prime (first) meridian, from which the others are measured, runs through Greenwich, England, near London. The prime meridian is at 0° (zero degrees) longitude. As it circles the other side of the earth it becomes 180° longitude, dividing the earth in half from north to south. East longitude is to the right of the prime meridian; west longitude is to the left.

1. On a globe of the earth find the prime meridian at the equator. Trace north on this line with your finger until you come to Greenwich, England.
2. On a world appendix map list the countries that the prime meridian passes through north of the equator.
3. Trace your finger completely around the globe from 0° prime meridian at Greenwich to 180° and back to Greenwich.

_____

_____

_____

Map Activity Quiz 5: Latitude and Longitude   Name: _____

You will need: Points: _____5_____

    Appendix Map 33, 34, or 35
    Globe
    Atlas

When latitude and longitude lines are overlaid on a globe or map, they form a grid. Since the earth is spheric or shaped like a ball, the distances on the grid are measured in degrees. A circle has 360°. The earth is circular at the equator and at the prime meridian. Having these lines fixed in place helps us to measure distances from one part of the earth to the other and to locate places more easily.

Using a globe or atlas, find the countries and cities that are in the following latitudes and longitudes. On a world appendix map, write their names approximately where they are located.

1. Countries
   50° north latitude, 15° east longitude
   30° north latitude, 30° west longitude
   25° south latitude, 135° east longitude
   35° north latitude, 25° east longitude
2. Cities
   30° north latitude, 90° west longitude
   26° south latitude, 28° east longitude
   35° north latitude, 90° west longitude
   25° north latitude, 67° east longitude
3. Find the approximate latitude and longitude where you live and place the name of the town or city on your map.

_____

_____

_____

_____

Map Activity Quiz 6: Weather

You will need:

Appendix Maps 4 and 5
Encyclopedia
Atlas

Name: _____

Points: _____5_____

Never a day goes by that we are not affected by the weather. The weather determines what we wear and whether we will need heat or air conditioning in our homes. It determines the type of recreation we engage in, the price of certain foods in the market, and even if those foods will be available to us.

Newspapers, radio, and television are our means of learning if the weather will allow schools to open, what the traffic patterns will be like on the highways, and what the weather is like in other parts of the country. We watch and listen to the weather reports to get some idea of how to plan the next few hours or days of activity.

1. Using the weather map from your daily newspaper as a guide, draw the various weather conditions around the country on Appendix Map 4. List below the states where the weather is rainy or snowy.

2. From the weather report in your daily newspaper find the five cities with the highest temperatures and the five with the lowest. Place these cities properly on Appendix Map 5 and indicate their high and low temperatures.

3. Study the weather information in your local newspaper and give a report to your class on what you learned. Use an encyclopedia for background information and an appendix map to illustrate what you found.

_____

_____

_____

_____

You will need:

Appendix Map 6

Name: _____

Points: ___5_____

As the earth rotates on its axis, it brings the United States into the bright rays of the sun once every 24 hours. The first people in the United States to see the sun are those living on the east coast. The rest of the country is still in darkness. Time zones were devised to accommodate people in each part of the country. After all, if it is 7 o'clock in the morning in the east, it will be three more hours before the earth's rotation allows the west coast to get the early morning sun. Most people would not be happy waiting until 10 o'clock in the morning for the sun to shine.

Answer the following questions at the bottom of this Map Activity Quiz.

1. If it is 7 A.M. in Ohio, what time is it in Wyoming?
2. If it is 3 P.M. in Minnesota, what time is it in most of Texas?
3. If the Rose Bowl football game starts at 4 P.M. (east coast time) on January 1, what time will it start in your part of the country?
4. What time zone has the fewest states or parts of states in it?
5. What time zone has the largest number of states or parts of states in it?

_____

_____

_____

_____

47

Map Activity Quiz 8: Traveling

You will need:

Name: _____

Points: ____5____

Travel advertisements from newspapers and magazines
Selected appendix maps
Reference maps
Encyclopedia

Every week newspapers and magazines advertise exotic places of interest to visit. From these sources choose any five places from around the world that you would like to visit. Ask your teacher for the appendix map or maps you need.

1. In the spaces below list each place you would like to visit and what you would expect to see and do there. Get your information from an advertisement or encyclopedia and other reference materials.
2. After finding the places you have selected on reference maps, locate them on your outline map or maps.
3. List on the map the name of the state or country, its capital, population, and the language spoken there (if it is out of the continental United States). You may need to check an encyclopedia or other reference materials to determine your answers.
4. Determine the cost of a vacation to the one place you like best. Include travel expenses to and from the airport, airline travel, meals, hotels, tips, and other expenses.

_____

_____

_____

_____

Map Activity Quiz 9: Canada

You will need:

    Appendix Map 20
    Atlas

Name: _____

Points: _____5_____

Canada is the second largest country in the world, 3,851,809 square miles. The northern part is hilly, a wilderness of lakes, forests, and frozen land. The east has rolling hills which become plains in the central section. Mountains rise abruptly in the west. In the south Canadians farm and find work in factories and mines. The border separating Canada from the United States is 3,987 miles long—the longest border in the world without a single fortification.

1. On Appendix Map 20 mark and place ten of Canada's largest cities:

    Montreal, Quebec   Ottawa, Ontario
    Toronto, Ontario   Winnipeg, Manitoba
    Edmonton, Alberta   Laval, Quebec
    Vancouver, British Columbia   London, Ontario
    Calgary, Alberta   Windsor, Ontario
    Hamilton, Ontario

2. On Appendix Map 20 label the Canadian provinces:

    Alberta   Ontario
    British Columbia   Prince Edward Island
    Manitoba   Quebec
    New Brunswick   Saskatchewan
    Newfoundland   Yukon
    Northwest Territories
    Nova Scotia

3. Mark and label the following on Appendix Map 20:

    Highest mountain—
        Mt. Logan   19,850 feet
    Longest river—
        Mackenzie   2,636 miles
    Largest island—
        Baffin Island   183,810 square miles

_____

_____

_____

_____

49

The Map Corner

Map Activity Quiz 10: Mexico

You will need:

Appendix Map 21
Atlas
Encyclopedia

Name: _____

Points: _____5_____

Mexico, with an area of 761,600 square miles, is a country about three times the size of Texas. Mexico has two peninsulas; Lower California to the west and the Yucatán Peninsula that juts out into the Gulf of Mexico. Mountain ranges form a giant wishbone around the outer edges of Mexico, enclosing a large central plateau. The Gulf of Mexico and the Pacific Ocean are only 134 miles apart at the Isthmus of Tehuantepec. The border separating Mexico from the United States is 2,013 miles long.

1. On Appendix Map 21 mark and place ten of Mexico's cities:

   Mexico City   Nuevo Laredo
   Guadalajara   Tijuana
   Monterrey   Tampico
   Puebla   Mérida
   Ciudad Juárez   Oaxaco

2. On Appendix Map 21 label the following mountain ranges:
   Sierra Madre Oriental
   Sierra Madre Occidental
   Sierra Madre del Sur

3. On Appendix Map 21 draw the Inter-American Highway from Laredo, Texas to Guatemala.

_____

_____

_____

_____

50

Map Activity Quiz 11: Central America

Name: _____

You will need:

Points: _____5_____

    Appendix Map 24
    Reference map of Central America

      Central America is a narrow land area connecting the Northern Hemisphere with the Southern Hemisphere. Seven countries make up this part of the world. These countries lie between 75° and 95° west longitude and 5° and 20° north latitude.

      Answer these questions on the spaces below or on Appendix Map 24.

1. What two countries border Mexico?
2. What direction would you travel if you entered the Panama Canal at Colón and exited at Panamá?
3. What large bodies of water are separated by Central America?
4. List the countries of Central America in alphabetical order and place their names within the outlines of the countries on Appendix Map 24.
5. Place an X where the capital of each country is located and write its name alongside.

_____

_____

_____

_____

51

The Map Corner

Map Activity Quiz 12: Australia

Name: _____

You will need:

Points: _____5_____

    Appendix Map 41
    Reference map of Australia
    Globe
    Encyclopedia

Australia is the continent "down under." If you look on a globe of the world, you will find it in the southwest section of the Pacific, directly south of China and Japan. This is the only country of the world that covers a whole continent by itself. It is almost as large as the United States, excluding Alaska and Hawaii.

1. Mark on Appendix Map 41 the location of the Great Barrier Reef. Find out what it is in an encyclopedia or reference book. Write your answer below.
2. Fill in the names of the states in Australia on your map. One state is off the south coast and is not shown on Appendix Map 41. Draw the outline of the state correctly and label it.
3. Four seas and two oceans surround Australia. List them on your map in the correct locations.
4. Place the names of the following cities in their correct locations on the map:

   Adelaide   Perth
   Melbourne   Hobart
   Sydney   Canberra
   Brisbane   Australian Capital Territory
5. Read about the Australian Capital Territory. To what does it compare in the United States?

_____

_____

_____

_____

52

Map Activity Quiz 13: The Middle East

You will need:

Name: _____

Points: _____5_____

Appendix Map 48
Reference map of the Middle East
Encyclopedia

The countries of what is known as the Middle East are constantly in the news. By using a reference map and an appendix map of the area, you will soon become familiar with countries in that part of the world.

1. Print the names of the following bodies of water or countries in their proper places on Appendix Map 48: Mediterranean Sea, Cyprus, Turkey, Iraq, Syria, Lebanon, Israel, Jordan, Saudi Arabia, and Egypt.
2. With a blue crayon or pencil fill in the boundaries and label the Sea of Galilee, Jordan River, Dead Sea, Gulf of Aqaba, Red Sea, Gulf of Suez, Nile River, and the route of the Suez Canal.
3. Using an encyclopedia or other reference aid, make a fact summary of each country. Include the following information:

land area   religion
climate   capital
population   form of government
language   monetary unit

_____

_____

_____

_____

53

The Explorer Series:
The Makers and Users of Maps

MARCO POLO 1254–1323

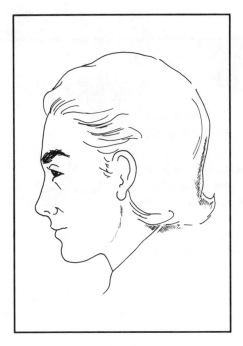

Marco Polo at seventeen
(artist's conception)

Venice was a great center of trade in the 1200s. As a young man Marco Polo watched as ships filled with merchandise sailed down the Adriatic to the eastern end of the Mediterranean Sea. Jewelry, glass, iron, and other materials were traded for spices, rugs, and gold that came overland from as far away as China.

Marco's father, Nicolo, and his uncle, Maffeo, took Marco to China on one of their trading expeditions when he was 17. At that time, the king who ruled most of the area between Europe and China was Kublai Khan. To get to the Kahn's kingdom the Polos had to cross deserts in Persia (now Iran) and Afghanistan and the Pamir Mountains in the southern part of the Soviet Union. They descended the mountains to Kashgar (Sufu) and Yarkand (Soche), trading cities in western China, crossed the burning Gobi Desert, and finally traveled to Cambaluc (now Peking) where Kublai Kahn had his court.

The Khan enjoyed the young Marco Polo very much and trusted him. Marco, who was proficient in learning languages, worked as a special aide to the Khan for many years. Marco traveled throughout the Khan's kingdom and had many adventures. For three years he even governed Yanchow south of Peking, a city of a quarter million people. When Marco was 40 years old, the Khan finally let him, his father, and his uncle return to Venice. They went back with costly silks. Within their traveling clothes they sewed such precious stones as sapphires, emeralds, diamonds, and rubies. They returned by ship past Indochina through the Indian Ocean. They finally arrived in Venice, after being away for 24 years. Marco was now in his early forties. While he and his father and uncle were traveling home, the Khan died, ending trade with China for many years.

Some time later Venice and Genoa were at war with each other. Marco, who captained a warship, was captured and thrown into prison. While there, as a way of passing the time, he spent hours telling the other prisoners fabulous stories of his adventures. A prisoner named Rustician suggested Marco put his adventures in writing. So Marco dictated his travels and adventures to Rustician, who copied them down by hand. They called the book *The Travels of Marco Polo*. It was recopied many times by hand and became very popular. Later, after the invention of the printing press, it was printed and distributed to many lands. Marco Polo became known as the "father of geography" because of the accuracy of his geographic descriptions.

Columbus read Marco Polo's book nearly two centuries later. The book influenced him to try to find a more direct, shorter, and, consequently, westerly route to China and India. Instead, he discovered America.

The Map Corner

As a young man Marco Polo went to China with his father and uncle on a trading expedition. Marco became a favorite of the ruler of China, Kublai Khan, and worked for him for many years. When Marco finally came home to Venice he was a rich man. Soon after his return he was thrown into prison where he dictated his adventures to a fellow prisoner. The tale of his travels became a book which has influenced many people. Columbus, in particular, became interested in a route to China by sailing west after reading Marco Polo's book.

1. Find a map in an encyclopedia or reference book that shows Marco Polo's trips. On a globe, trace the routes with your finger.

2. On Appendix Map 33, mark and label the places he went to on his journeys. Use an atlas to help you in your search of the following places:

Venice	Afghanistan	Indochina
Adriatic Sea	Pamir Mountains	Indian Ocean
Mediterranean Sea	Kashgar	Venice
Iran	Yarkand	Genoa
	Peking	

3. Prepare an oral report on Marco Polo, using an encyclopedia or book your librarian might suggest. Outline what you are going to say in the space below. Give your report in class using your map to illustrate the route Marco Polo took.

_____

_____

_____

_____

CHRISTOPHER COLUMBUS 1451–1506

Christopher Columbus

The discovery of America was an accident!

Christopher Columbus, born in Genoa, Italy, and whose name is spelled Cristoforo Colombo in Italian, was actually trying to find a westward route from Europe to Asia. When he sighted land he thought he had, since he used Ptolemy's calculation of the earth's circumference—18,000 miles. By Columbus' reckoning he was there.

For a while, Columbus aligned himself with the Portuguese, since, at that time, they were the world's greatest seafaring nation. He learned the Portuguese language; he also learned Latin, so he could read the scholarly geographies of that time, and Castilian, the official language of Spain. He even became a chartmaker. All of this study was in preparation for Columbus' journey to Asia, sailing west. He was convinced that this was the route to take.

But Portugal, under King John II, did not hold the same view. The Portuguese were convinced the sea route should be around the southern tip of Africa and then east to Asia. So Columbus' request for a ship was denied.

Columbus then went to Spain. At that time the Spanish were involved in a war with the Moors in Granada. Finally, after many petitions from Columbus, Queen Isabella was convinced that Spain would gain much by sending him west across the Atlantic. She even went so far as to offer her jewels to finance the trip. A little town on Cape Palos, which had incurred the displeasure of the Spanish government, was made to build two ships, the *Niña* and *Pinta.* The *Santa Maria* was loaned to the government for the trip.

On August 3, 1492 the three ships left Palos harbor and sailed to the Canary Islands. They immediately ran into trouble. The *Pinta* needed a new rudder, and the *Niña* needed different sails. After repairs, they sailed west for about a month; the crew became discouraged. Columbus urged them to keep on with him. When they sighted weeds, berries, and a carved board in the sea, the crew was encouraged. Soon land was sighted—San Salvador!

The *Santa Maria* ran aground, so Columbus built a small fort from the lumber of the ship. Many of the crew were enchanted with the islands. They thought they would become rich with gold if they stayed in the New World until Columbus could come back for them. They begged to stay, so Columbus left 39 men behind and returned to Spain. When he came back all the men had been killed.

Columbus was now famous, honored, and wealthy. He returned to the Americas three more times. On the last trip he explored along the east coast of Central America. Although he could not get through, he died thinking he had reached Asia.

59

The Map Corner

Map Activity Quiz 15: Christopher Columbus   Name: _____

You will need: Points: _____5_____

    Appendix Maps 23 and 33
    Atlas
    Encyclopedia
    National Geographic, November 1975, Vol. 148, No. 5

Christopher Columbus was convinced from his studies of geography that a person could sail west and land in Asia, where great wealth could be gotten through trade. Turned down by the Portuguese, who were more interested in an eastward route around Africa, he turned to Spain for support. Ferdinand and Isabella agreed and eventually he got three ships, the *Niña, Pinta,* and *Santa Maria.*

On October 12, 1492 he put ashore on the island of San Salvador. He made three more trips and died believing he had reached Asia.

1. Read the article in the Explorer Series on Christopher Columbus. Label on Appendix Map 33 Columbus' birth place (Genoa, Italy); also, Spain, Cape Palos, Portugal, the Canary Islands, and his Atlantic route to San Salvador. Use your atlas to help you.
   Do either 2 or 3.
2. Turn to pages 595, 602, 612, and 614 in the November 1975 *National Geographic.* Trace the four voyages of Columbus on Appendix Map 23 in different colors and label the major islands.
3. Read about Columbus in an encyclopedia and other books suggested by your librarian. Prepare a written report on his life and travels.

_____

_____

_____

_____

VASCO DA GAMA 1460–1524

Vasco da Gama

For many years men had sailed down the west coast of Africa, always forced to stop along the way because of treacherous winds and currents. King Emanuel I of Portugal finally decided to send a fleet all the way around Africa to India. His choice of leader was Vasco da Gama.

Vasco da Gama was a good selection. He was courageous but often merciless. His violent anger kept his men in fear of him. The dangerous trip required a leader who would not turn back. Most people at that time in history were superstitious, and a trip into unknown waters would have made them fearful.

With his brother Paulo in charge of one of the four ships and a crew of 170, da Gama sailed from Lisbon on July 8, 1497. Da Gama set a course into the South Atlantic, far around the winds and currents of the west coast of Africa. He actually came close to finding South America. His ships were out of sight of land for thousands of miles—over three months. The stars and constellations were unfamiliar to them in the South Atlantic.

Scurvy made the hands and feet of the crew swell. Their gums became swollen, covering their teeth. Then storms hit them. The men pleaded with da Gama to return to Portugal, but he kept his course and by November they rounded the Cape of Good Hope.

After 11 months they reached India. They landed at Calicut, now known as Kozhikode, in the southwest part of India. They spent a few months there and then began the long voyage home.

Off the coast of India the ships were surrounded by pirates in 70 boats. The wind had ceased and Vasco's ships were becalmed. When the pirates drew close da Gama ordered his men to shoot their cannons. At that moment the wind began to blow and although they were pursued for a while, the ships managed to get away in a thunderstorm.

Not everyone survived the harsh trip. Of the 170 men who boarded the ships many months before, only 55 were left. Vasco buried his brother in the Azores before reaching Lisbon.

Vasco da Gama had been away for two years. Upon his return he received honors and wealth. He made two more trips to India. On his last journey he went as viceroy but died soon after arriving at Cochin, India. He had truly united the East and West.

Map Activity Quiz 16: Vasco da Gama   Name: _____

You will need: Points: _____5_____

    Appendix Map 33
    Atlas
    Globe

Vasco da Gama is described by some historians as a short, heavyset man with a hot temper and a haughty, pitiless, domineering attitude. He probably needed all those qualities and more to take a crew of superstitious men into the South Atlantic, around the Cape of Good Hope, and into waters sailed by pirates to find a sea route to India. However, he did make the voyage, which up until his time had been impossible, and, subsequently, found a sea route to India from East to West.

1. On Appendix Map 33 label the cities and places where Vasco da Gama lived or had sailed to: Sines, Portugal (just south of Lisbon on the coast) where he was born; Lisbon; Canary Islands; Azores; Cape Verde Islands; Cape of Good Hope; and Calicut, in India.

2. Prepare a short report on Vasco da Gama, using the article in the Explorer Series, an encyclopedia, or a book your librarian might suggest. Give an oral report in class using your map and a globe to illustrate the voyage he took to India. Use the space below to outline your talk.

_____

_____

_____

_____

FERDINAND MAGELLAN 1480–1521

Ferdinand Magellan

One of the most fearless explorers who ever lived was a Portuguese sailor named Ferdinand Magellan. His loyalty to his men was boundless and in the end this loyalty resulted in his death. He was known as a fierce fighting man with a mind of his own. At one time he disobeyed his commanders and took a crew from India to the Spice Islands, which are the Moluccas. He gave up his Portuguese citizenship to sail for Charles V of Spain.

King Charles supported Magellan's ambition to sail around the world. He was given five ships and left Seville, Spain on August 10, 1519. The trip was marked by mutiny, extreme cold, lack of food and water, and unfriendly natives.

From Seville, Magellan and his crews crossed the Atlantic to South America. At San Julián (the Atlantic side of southernmost Argentina) three of his captains mutinied. Magellan was able to overcome them and then continue around the lower tip of South America. This difficult passageway became known as the Straits of Magellan. The trip was extremely hazardous and resulted in one ship returning to Spain and another being wrecked.

Finally, after rounding what is now Cape Horn, Magellan and his men were met by a broad expanse of ocean. He named it *Pacific* because of its apparent calm and peacefulness.

Sailing north along the coast of what is now Chile, Magellan then turned west to cross the Pacific. Their food gone and the water putrid, the sailors ate the rats they found on ship and even ate the leather used to lash down the sails. Over three months passed and finally they came to Theive's Island, which is now Guam. Continuing on they made their way through the Philippines to an island called *Cebu.*

Magellan made friends with the people and the king of Cebu. Unknown to Magellan, the king was using him to attain more power. Magellan was taken in by this duplicity and led a raiding party to another island. Here Magellan was killed helping some of his men escape.

Three years had gone by. Of the five ships that set sail from Seville, Spain, only one returned. Sebastián del Camo took command on the remaining ship, *Victoria.* Spices were loaded into the ship in the Moluccas and then captain and crew headed for home around the Cape of Good Hope. The voyage began with 265 men; 18 survived.

Magellan had sailed around the world. An earlier trip had taken him beyond the longitude where he landed in the Philippines. He had overlapped his first trip and attained the great ambition of his life of circumnavigating the earth.

The Map Corner

Map Activity Quiz 17: Ferdinand Magellan

You will need:

Appendix Map 33 or 34
Atlas
Encyclopedia

Name: _____

Points: _____5_____

Ferdinand Magellan's great ambition was to sail around the world. Although he was not able to do it on one continuous voyage, he did manage to get half way around twice by going in two different directions on two separate trips. He is generally given credit for being the first to circle the earth.

1. Find the approximate longitude Magellan attained on his first voyage to the Spice Islands or Moluccas and the approximate longitude of his later trip to Cebu in the Philippines. Mark these longitude lines on Appendix Map 33. You may use an atlas and encyclopedia to help you.
2. Using an encyclopedia, trace on Appendix Map 34 the trip of Magellan and his crew around the world beginning at Seville, Spain.
3. Label these locations on Appendix Map 33 or 34.

   Seville, Spain   Thieve's Island (Guam)
   Spice Islands (Moluccas)   Pacific Ocean
   South America   Atlantic Ocean
   San Julián   Philippine Islands
   Straits of Magellan   Cebu
       (Estrecho de Magallanes)   India
   Cape Horn   Africa
   Chile   Cape of Good Hope

_____

_____

_____

_____

SIR WALTER RALEIGH 1552-1618

Sir Walter Raleigh

Explorer, sailor, soldier, historian, colonizer, poet, and politician—such were the talents of Sir Walter Raleigh. Born in Devonshire, England, he went to college at Oxford University, just 52 miles northwest of London. After three years of study he decided to go to France. At that time the French Protestants, called Huguenots, were at war with the Catholics. Raleigh enjoyed a fight and threw himself into it. Later, he went to Ireland to battle and distinguished himself there as a soldier.

Elizabeth I, Queen of England, enjoyed Raleigh. He wrote poetry for her and even laid his velvet coat over a puddle of mud so she would not get her satin shoes dirty. She was impressed! Later she knighted him and gave him patents, which meant wine and cloth makers had to pay him a fee for their licenses. With this source of income he became very wealthy. His great ambition was to sail to North and South America and see the land colonized by Englishmen. However, because of her fondness for him and the amusement he gave her, Queen Elizabeth wanted Sir Walter close by her in court.

Raleigh had to be content to send others on these trips. One expedition claimed Newfoundland for England. Another colonized Roanoke, an island off the coast of North Carolina. Here the first English child to be born in America, Virginia Dare, entered the world on August 18, 1587. Unfortunately, the colonists disappeared during a three-year wait for supplies from England. No one knows what happened to them. Raleigh then named another area Virginia, which eventually became the state of Virginia. (Elizabeth I was known as the "Virgin Queen" since she never married.) Raleigh, the capital of North Carolina, was named after Sir Walter.

Finally, the Queen allowed Raleigh to take ships in search of the Lost City of Gold—El Dorado. In 1595, he sailed to Lisbon, Portugal, on through the Canary Islands, then to Trinidad, an island off the coast of Venezuela. He sailed up the Orinoco River in Venezuela only to be disappointed. There was no El Dorado.

Raleigh had made many enemies throughout his life. As a result, he spent a number of years in the Tower of London as a prisoner. When Queen Elizabeth died her cousin James of Scotland succeeded her. In 1616 Raleigh asked King James to free him to search for gold. King James released Raleigh from prison after he had spent twelve and a half years there. He was now an old man but the chance to sail was again given him.

He sailed from England to Ireland, south to the Cape Verde Islands, and again to the Orinoco River. He disobeyed King James by engaging in battle with the Spanish. The trip ended in tragedy when Raleigh lost his son in an ambush.

On his return home, Raleigh's enemies plotted against him. King James had him beheaded at the Tower of London so England could stay in Spain's good graces.

The Map Corner

Sir Walter Raleigh was a many-talented man. As a politician and colonizer he made England more aware of the potential of the Northern and Southern Hemispheres. His friendship with Elizabeth I, Queen of England, allowed him to attempt to colonize America. Although colonization was not immediately successful, the English eventually became the dominant force in the Northern Hemisphere, partly as a result of Raleigh's efforts.

1. On Appendix Map 43 label Devonshire, the town where Sir Walter Raleigh was born, and the capital of England, London. Draw in the Thames River. Label the areas of England, Scotland, Wales, Ireland, and Northern Ireland.

2. Sir Walter Raleigh was involved in the following areas of the world: Newfoundland, Virginia, Roanoke Island, Raleigh, North Carolina, Lisbon, Portugal, the Canary Islands, Trinidad, Venezuela, the Orinoco River, and the Cape Verde Islands. Label them on Appendix Map 29 and 33.

3. Read about Sir Walter Raleigh in your textbook, encyclopedia, or other reference materials. List below the various talents he had and any other interesting things you may have found out about him.

_____

_____

_____

_____

66

HENRY HUDSON 1575-1611

Henry Hudson

During the 1600s there were a number of attempts made to find a route to China and Japan by way of the Northern Hemisphere where Canada and the North Polar Ice Cap meet. The best known explorer to try this was Henry Hudson, who made four major voyages into the northern areas.

His first trip in 1607 took him from England to the northeast coast of Greenland, then to Spitzbergen (now Svalbard), south to Bear Island, on to Jan Mayen Island (which he accidentally discovered), and then home again up the Thames River in England.

The second voyage in 1608 took him and his crew past the North Cape of Norway in an effort to discover an open path through the Barents Sea between Svalbard and Novaya Zemlya. He had to return to England in frustration because the way was blocked by ice.

The third trip in 1609 took him first to Newfoundland, then to the Kennebec River (in what is now the state of Maine), and then farther south to the river that bears his name, the Hudson River. Although he was not the first European to discover the river, he was the first to sail up it for any distance. He actually sailed to what is now the capital of New York State, Albany. Little did he realize that, in the future, one of the greatest cities and harbors in the world, New York City and New York Harbor, would welcome many peoples from all over the world.

After returning home, he was commissioned in 1612 to make another attempt to find the elusive passageway across the northern part of the world. This last time he sailed from London to Iceland, below Greenland, through the Davis Strait in upper Canada, and then around the edges of a large bay, which also carries his name, Hudson Bay.

The ship's crew mutinied and left Henry Hudson, his son, the ship's carpenter, and six sick crewmen adrift in a small boat. No one knows for sure what happened to Hudson, his son, and his men.

Map Activity Quiz 19: Henry Hudson   Name: _____

You will need: Points: _____5_____

    Appendix Maps 25 and 31
    Atlas
    Encyclopedia

      Henry Hudson made four attempts to find a sea route from Europe across the North Polar Ice Cap. Although he was unable to find a route, he contributed a great deal to our knowledge of the region. The Hudson River and Hudson's Bay in Canada are continual reminders of this explorer's work.

1. Trace the general routes of Henry Hudson's voyages on Appendix Maps 25 and 31. Use different colored pens, pencils, or crayons for each trip and mark the year the trip was taken. Use an encyclopedia, atlas, or other reference books to find the locations.
2. Prepare a short report on Henry Hudson, using an encyclopedia or book your librarian might suggest. Give an oral report in class using your maps to illustrate the various trips Hudson took. Use the space below to outline your talk.

_____

_____

_____

_____

68

CAPTAIN JAMES COOK 1728-1779

Captain James Cook

As a young Englishman, James Cook was enchanted with the sea. His first experience was on ships carrying coal and supplies to the towns along the coast of England in the area of the North Sea. When he was 27, he decided to join the British Navy.

Cook's first assignment was to chart the St. Lawrence River near Quebec in Canada during a battle with the French. This he did successfully and then went on to chart the coastline of Nova Scotia. He spent the next eight years making charts of the northern coast of North America.

A scholarly paper he wrote on an eclipse of the sun brought him recognition among scientists. He was given the assignment of taking a scientific expedition from England to Tahiti in 1768 to record the 1769 eclipse of the planet Venus as it passed across the face of the sun.

As captain of the ship *Endeavour*, he ordered his men to eat onions as a way of preventing scurvy. Scurvy is a disease which makes gums swell and bleed. A person gets red splotches over the skin and becomes exhausted. It is caused by a lack of vitamin C. Captain Cook also provided his men with sauerkraut and fruit, which was much different from the standard sea fare of biscuits and salt meat. Since scurvy was no problem on his ship, as it was on others, he could sail farther and not be delayed by men who were continuously sick.

Cook sailed on to New Zealand and Australia and had many fascinating adventures. He took his crew around the Great Barrier Reef along the northeast coast of Australia, across the Indian Ocean, below Cape Town at the southern tip of Africa, and then north to England.

Captain Cook's fame as an explorer grew. His charts and notes had made him quite famous, so the British Royal Navy sent him on a second voyage in 1772. This time he was to explore the South Pole. He sailed to Cape Town and then south, close to Antarctica (discovered in 1821), east along the southernmost part of the Indian Ocean to New Zealand, on into the South Seas where he charted more islands, and then to Easter Island, which had been discovered on Easter Day in 1722 by a Dutch Admiral.

His third and last major voyage began in July, 1776, when he was 48. Cook had orders to try to find a passageway across the top of North America. Cook chose to sail around Africa and then on to Australia and New Zealand. Just before Christmas he sighted an island in the Pacific. He called it Christmas Island. A short time later he came across a group of islands that he named the Sandwich Islands in honor of the Earl of Sandwich, the first lord of the Admiralty in England. They are now called the Hawaiian Islands and are part of the United States.

In 1778 he reached the coastline of North America, at a spot where the state of Oregon is now located. He sailed north to the Aleutian Islands in search of a passageway across the top of the world. The effort was fruitless. After sailing to the Bering Strait, he returned to Hawaii. He was killed by natives while fighting over a stolen boat.

The Map Corner

Map Activity Quiz 20: Captain James Cook

You will need:

    Appendix Map 33
    Atlas
    Encyclopedia

Name: _____

Points: _____5_____

Captain James Cook spent most of his life with one thought in mind—to explore and map the world. He was a mathematician, marine surveyor, and something of a practical physician. His insights into the dietary needs of sailors brought him honors because he had his crew eat sauerkraut, onions, and fruit on his voyages. None of his men got scurvy, which had proved so disastrous to men on other vessels. Captain Cook made it easier for men to sail and to find the destinations for which they were looking.

1. Captain Cook made three major voyages. Read about them from the Explorer Series or an encyclopedia. Trace them on Appendix Map 33 in different colors of crayon or pencil. Label on your map the places Captain Cook visited.

2. Find Easter Island on a map of the world. Determine its longitude and latitude. Read in an encyclopedia or a book your librarian might recommend about the giant statues there, how they were formed, and how they were transported to their present locations. Make notes in the space below and then report to your class on what you found.

_____

_____

_____

_____

MERIWETHER LEWIS 1774-1809 WILLIAM CLARK 1770-1838

Lewis and Clark

As young boys Meriwether Lewis and William Clark played and hunted together. Their friendship grew over the years. When Thomas Jefferson, President of the United States, decided to send an expedition into the northwest section of our country, he turned to his young secretary, Meriwether Lewis, as a volunteer. Lewis was delighted and asked for Clark as a coleader. Jefferson complied. The president was concerned that our country would not have enough room for expansion in the future. At this time the Mississippi was our western border. He also wanted peace with the Indians and a mapping of the waterways in the west.

The expedition learned just before they set out from St. Louis that they would be exploring American land. In 1803, Napolean of France sold a great amount of territory to the United States. This was called the Louisiana Purchase. Lewis and Clark were to be the first Americans to explore this territory to the Pacific Ocean.

On May 14, 1804 they started up the Missouri River. At the end of July they had their first meeting with Indians at Council Bluffs, Iowa. They pushed on to what is presently Stanton, North Dakota, where they spent the winter with the Mandan Indians. Here they met and hired a French interpreter, Toussaint Charbonneau. His wife was a Shoshone Indian called Sacajawea, or Bird Woman. Sacajawea proved to be more helpful than her husband to the expedition.

Having encountered many difficulties of sickness, portage around river falls and over mountains, and many other obstacles, they finally crossed the Continental Divide and descended the Columbia River to the Pacific Ocean.

On their way back, the expedition split to gather more information about the country. Clark headed for Yellowstone River and followed it along to the Missouri River. Lewis took a group of men on an exploration of a branch of the Missouri which he called Marias. Later, the parties joined again and arrived in St. Louis, Missouri on September 23, 1806. Their trip covered 6,000 miles and lasted two years, four months, and nine days.

The Map Corner

Map Activity Quiz 21: Lewis and Clark

Name: _____

You will need:

Points: _____5_____

Appendix Maps 4 and 5
Atlas
Encyclopedia
History textbook

Lewis and Clark were close friends as young men. They hunted together for racoon and possum. Later in life they were brought together when President Jefferson asked his young secretary, Meriwether Lewis, to head an expedition to the Northwest. Lewis asked that his old friend, William Clark, be coleader with him.

They headed up the Missouri River from St. Louis. Lewis had prepared himself by studying maps and learning to find his position by latitude and longitude. He already knew much about plants and animals. Along the way he collected soil samples and kept an accurate log of his experiences. William Clark brought his military experience to the expedition. His older brother, George Rogers Clark, was a famous soldier. Clark's military knowledge and ability kept the expedition from disaster several times.

Their trip took over two years and covered 6,000 miles.

1. From an atlas, trace the following rivers on Appendix Map 4.
   Mississippi River
   Missouri River
   Snake River
   Columbia River
   Yellowstone River
2. Read the account of the Lewis and Clark expedition in your history text or encyclopedia and trace their travels to and from the Northwest on Appendix Map 4.
3. Read in your history text or encyclopedia about the Louisiana Purchase. Outline the boundaries of the Louisiana Purchase of 1803 on Appendix Map 5. Was your state included in any portion of that purchase? _____

AMELIA EARHART 1898–1937

Amelia Earhart

Amelia Earhart, like Magellan, had one obsession—to circle the earth. Only she wanted to do it by flying. She wrote in her book *Last Flight:* "There was one flight which I most wanted to attempt—a circumnavigation of the globe as near its waistline as could be."

Even as a young girl Amelia Earhart had an adventurous spirit. In the early 1900s flying was a sport and occupation dominated by men. But Amelia persevered. She took a job just to pay for her flying lessons. She was taught by one of the few women in the world who knew how to fly at that time, Neta Snook. Amelia's mother was interested enough to help her buy an airplane.

Amelia became the first woman to fly the Atlantic. Charles A. Lindberg, the first person to fly solo from the United States to Europe, encouraged her to make the trip with two men.

Because of her writing and flying, Amelia Earhart became well known and an inspiration to many women. She eventually did fly solo across the Atlantic from Newfoundland to Ireland, setting a new record at that time. In 1935 she became the first person to fly across the Pacific between Hawaii and California.

One evening in Washington, D.C., she invited Mrs. Eleanor Roosevelt, President Franklin D. Roosevelt's wife, for a flight over the Capitol. While in the air, Amelia took over the controls of the plane from the pilot. At the time, Amelia was wearing an evening gown, slippers, and white gloves!

However, Amelia's great desire was to fly around the world at the equator. Her first attempt was to fly west. This flight ended in the crash of her plane. She tried again by flying east. With her navigator, Fred Noonan, they left California for Miami, Florida. They flew to South America, then Africa, and on to India. Out in the Pacific they landed at Lae, New Guinea. Their next stop was to be Howland Island in the Pacific. Although there was some radio contact with her and the United States Coast Guard, Amelia and Fred Noonan apparently were lost at sea. Over the years since 1937, there have been many stories as to what happened to them. Some suggest they were captured by the Japanese Navy. All that is known for sure is that they disappeared, probably lost at sea.

73

Map Activity Quiz 22: Amelia Earhart

You will need:

    Appendix Map 33
    Atlas
    Encyclopedia
    Globe

Name: _____

Points: _____5_____

Amelia Earhart was the first well-known woman flyer. She set a number of flying records, but had the great ambition to fly around the earth "as near its waistline as could be." She nearly accomplished this ambition but was lost with her navigator in the Pacific Ocean. Her writing and accomplishments have been an inspiration to men and women to try to do the difficult and the uncommon.

1. On Appendix Map 33 trace the route of Amelia Earhart's flight around the earth. Put an X at each place where she stopped and write the name of the town or city. When you are finished go back and add the names of the countries where these places are located. You will need an atlas to help you. Listed below, in order of visitation, are the places that she flew to.

1. Oakland	11. Dakar	21. Akyab
2. Tucson	12. Gao	22. Rangoon
3. New Orleans	13. Fort Lamy	23. Bangkok
4. Miami	14. El Fasher	24. Singapore
5. San Juan	15. Khartoum	25. Bandung
6. Caripito	16. Massaua	26. Surabaya
7. Paramaribo	17. Assab	27. Kupang
8. Fortaleza	18. Gwadar	28. Port Darwin
9. Natal	19. Karachi	29. Lae
10. St. Louis	20. Calcutta	30. Unknown

2. Prepare a short report on Amelia Earhart, using the article on her from the Explorer Series, an encyclopedia, or a book your librarian might suggest. Give your report in class, using a globe and your map to illustrate the route she took.

_____

_____

_____

_____

WILEY POST
1899–1935

Wiley Post

Wiley Post, tired of his job of flying an employer to his oil fields, got permission to take time off to plan a "round-the-world" flight to stimulate nation-wide interest in flying. He and his navigator, Harold Gatty, planned to fly the *Winnie Mae* to make the dream come true. In 1923, two United States Army planes out of the four that had started together successfully made the round-the-world trip in 15 days, 3 hours, and 7 minutes. So Post, a pioneer high-altitude pilot, and his navigator decided to set a record for flying an airplane around the world.

Harold Gatty was an expert navigator. Gatty was to sit half-way back in the plane, behind the main gas tank. In the wings above were other gas tanks. Gatty determined their course through hatches built overhead and below his seat. Through the top hatch he charted their way by the stars, and through the bottom hatch he used a special drift-and-

speed indicator where all he needed to know was the altitude of the airplane above an object on the ground.

After much preparation the two men took off on Tuesday morning, June 23, 1931 at 8:55:21 from Roosevelt Field, Long Island, New York. Eight days, 15 hours, and 51 minutes later they returned to the same field as heroes! Wiley Post had satisfied a life-long ambition to fly around the earth.

Around the World in 8 Days became the title of a book Wiley Post and Harold Gatty later wrote. In it they described how they prepared for the trip and their experience during and after the flight. Interestingly, Wiley Post was handicapped. In 1925, several years before his historic flight, he lost his left eye in an oil-drilling accident. This did not keep him from flying, however.

Post continued to fly after his trip with Gatty. In 1933 he made the first solo round-the-world flight (15,596 miles) in 7 days, 18 hours, and 49 minutes. Two years later, on a flight to Alaska, he died in a plane crash with humorist Will Rogers.

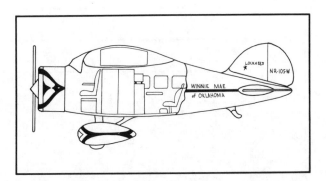

"Winnie Mae"

75

The Map Corner

Map Activity Quiz 23: Wiley Post

You will need:

    Appendix Map 33
    Atlas
    Globe

Name: _____

Points: _____5_____

Wiley Post was a pioneer high-altitude pilot, handicapped by an accident that required the removal of his left eye. He set a round-the-world flight record with his navigator, Harold Gatty. Later, he went on to become the first person to fly around the world by himself in a plane.

His record-setting flight with Harold Gatty took 8 days, 15 hours, and 51 minutes. Below are the cities where they landed for refueling and rest. On June 23, 1931 they took off from Roosevelt Field, Long Island, New York.

June 23 Harbor Grace, Newfoundland

June 24 Chester, England

June 24 Hannover, Germany

June 24 Berlin, Germany

June 25 Moscow, U.S.S.R.

June 26 Novosibirsk, U.S.S.R.

June 27 Irkutsk, U.S.S.R.

June 27 Blagoveshchensk, U.S.S.R.

June 28–29 Khabarovsk, U.S.S.R.

June 29 Nome, Alaska, U.S.A.

June 30 Fairbanks, Alaska, U.S.A.

July 1 Edmonton, Canada

July 1 Cleveland, Ohio, U.S.A.

July 1 return to Roosevelt Field

1. Trace their flight on a globe using an atlas for reference whenever needed.
2. Trace the flight on Appendix Map 33 and then label the cities where they landed for rest and refueling.
3. Label the countries where they landed and over which they crossed.

_____

_____

_____

_____

76

Appendix Maps

𝕿𝖍𝖎𝖘 𝖈𝖊𝖗𝖙𝖎𝖋𝖎𝖊𝖘 𝖙𝖍𝖆𝖙

_____

name

𝖍𝖆𝖘 𝖊𝖆𝖗𝖓𝖊𝖉 𝖙𝖍𝖎𝖘

𝕮𝖊𝖗𝖙𝖎𝖋𝖎𝖈𝖆𝖙𝖊 𝖔𝖋 𝕸𝖆𝖕 𝕾𝖐𝖎𝖑𝖑 𝕻𝖗𝖔𝖋𝖎𝖈𝖎𝖊𝖓𝖈𝖞

𝖆𝖘

_____

award

𝖎𝖓 𝖈𝖔𝖓𝖘𝖎𝖉𝖊𝖗𝖆𝖙𝖎𝖔𝖓 𝖔𝖋 𝖙𝖍𝖊 𝖘𝖆𝖙𝖎𝖘𝖋𝖆𝖈𝖙𝖔𝖗𝖞 𝖈𝖔𝖒𝖕𝖑𝖊𝖙𝖎𝖔𝖓
𝖔𝖋 𝖙𝖍𝖊 𝖈𝖔𝖚𝖗𝖘𝖊 𝖕𝖗𝖊𝖘𝖈𝖗𝖎𝖇𝖊𝖉 𝖎𝖓

𝕿𝖍𝖊 𝕸𝖆𝖕 𝕮𝖔𝖗𝖓𝖊𝖗

𝕴𝖓 𝖙𝖊𝖘𝖙𝖎𝖒𝖔𝖓𝖞 𝖜𝖍𝖊𝖗𝖊𝖔𝖋, 𝖙𝖍𝖊 𝕾𝖊𝖆𝖑 𝖔𝖋 𝖙𝖍𝖊 𝕮𝖔𝖒𝖕𝖆𝖘𝖘 𝕽𝖔𝖘𝖊
𝖆𝖓𝖉 𝖙𝖍𝖊 𝖘𝖎𝖌𝖓𝖆𝖙𝖚𝖗𝖊𝖘 𝖆𝖘 𝖆𝖚𝖙𝖍𝖔𝖗𝖎𝖟𝖊𝖉 𝖇𝖞 𝖙𝖍𝖊 𝖆𝖚𝖙𝖍𝖔𝖗𝖘
𝖆𝖗𝖊 𝖍𝖊𝖗𝖊𝖚𝖓𝖙𝖔 𝖆𝖋𝖋𝖎𝖝𝖊𝖉.

𝕲𝖎𝖛𝖊𝖓 𝖆𝖙 _____

school/organization

𝖔𝖓 𝖙𝖍𝖊 _____ 𝖔𝖋 _____ 𝖎𝖓 𝖙𝖍𝖊 𝖞𝖊𝖆𝖗 _____

day   month

Arnold B. Cheyney

Arnold B. Cheyney

University of Miami
Coral Gables, Florida

Donald L. Capone

Donald L. Capone

University of Miami
Coral Gables, Florida

_____

Course Instructor

_____

Tourist   Traveler   Navigator   Explorer   **79**

Instructor's Checklist for CERTIFICATE OF MAP SKILL PROFICIENCY

Each activity is worth 5 points. Place a checkmark in the appropriate box for each activity completed. For each student, add up the total number of activities checked off. This number multiplied by 5 equals the Total Point Score. The rating scale appears below.

Tourist (25 points)   **Traveler (50 points)**   **Navigator (75 points)**   **Explorer (100 points)**

Student's Name	Numbered Activities:	1	2	3	4	5	6	7	8	9	10	11	12	13	14	15	16	17	18	19	20	21	22	23	Total
1.																									
2.																									
3.																									
4.																									
5.																									
6.																									
7.																									
8.																									
9.																									
10.																									
11.																									
12.																									
13.																									
14.																									
15.																									
16.																									
17.																									
18.																									
19.																									
20.																									

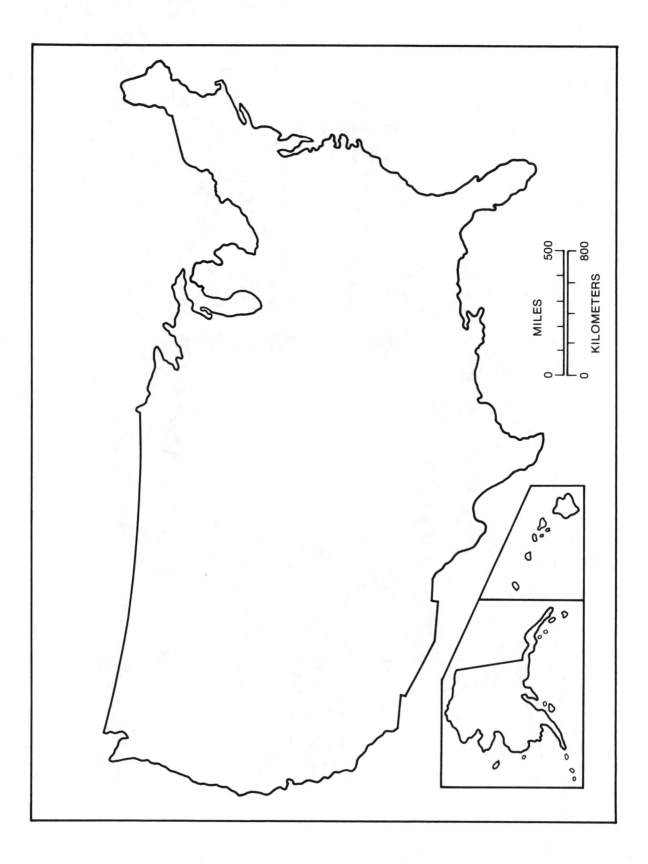

MILES

KILOMETERS

500

800

0

0

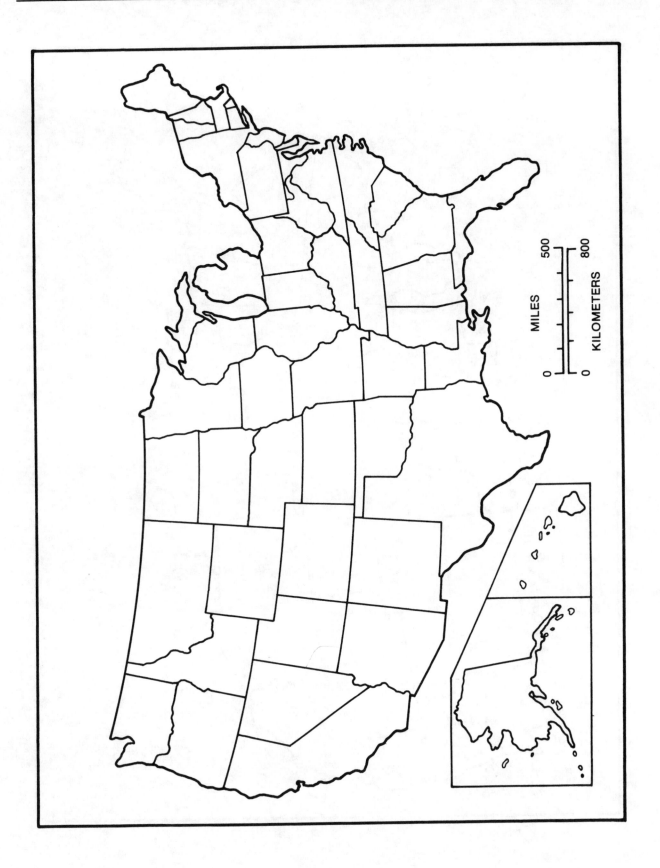

MILES

KILOMETERS

500

800

0

0

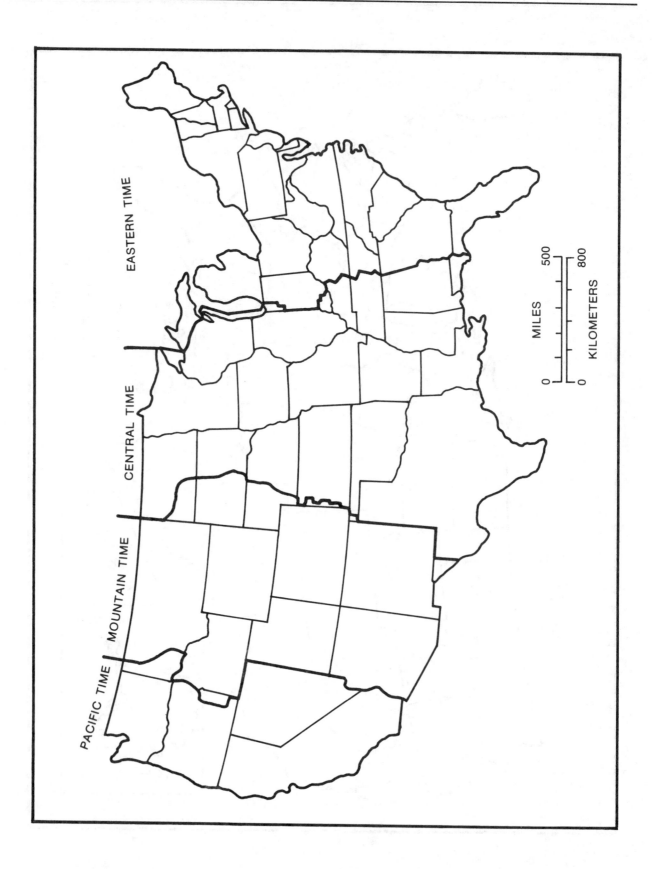

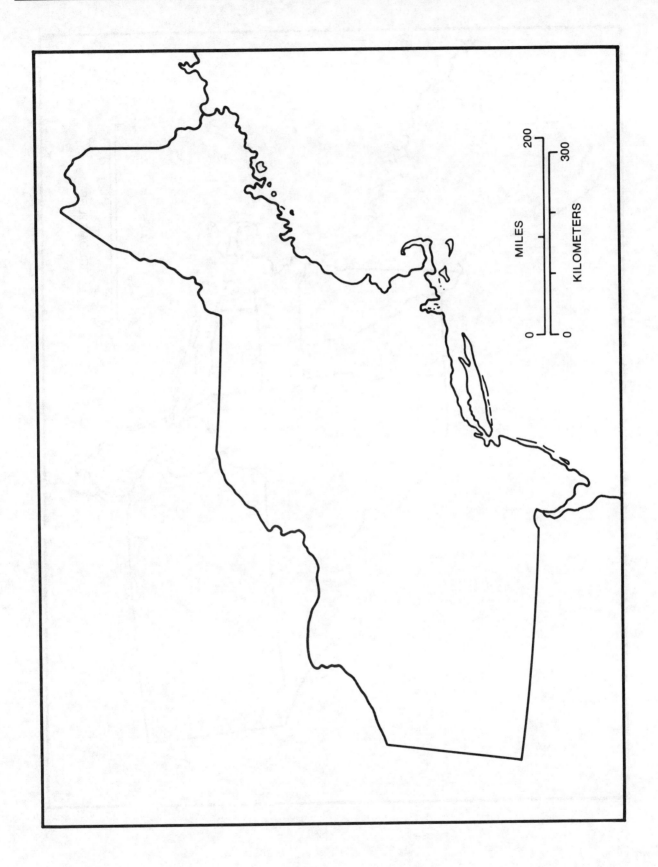

MILES

KILOMETERS

0 — 200

0 — 300

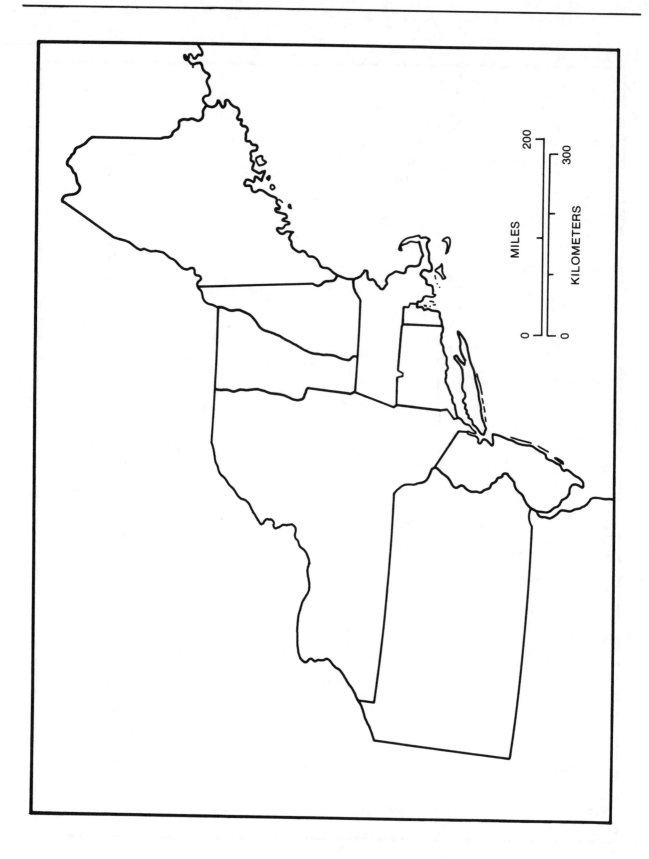

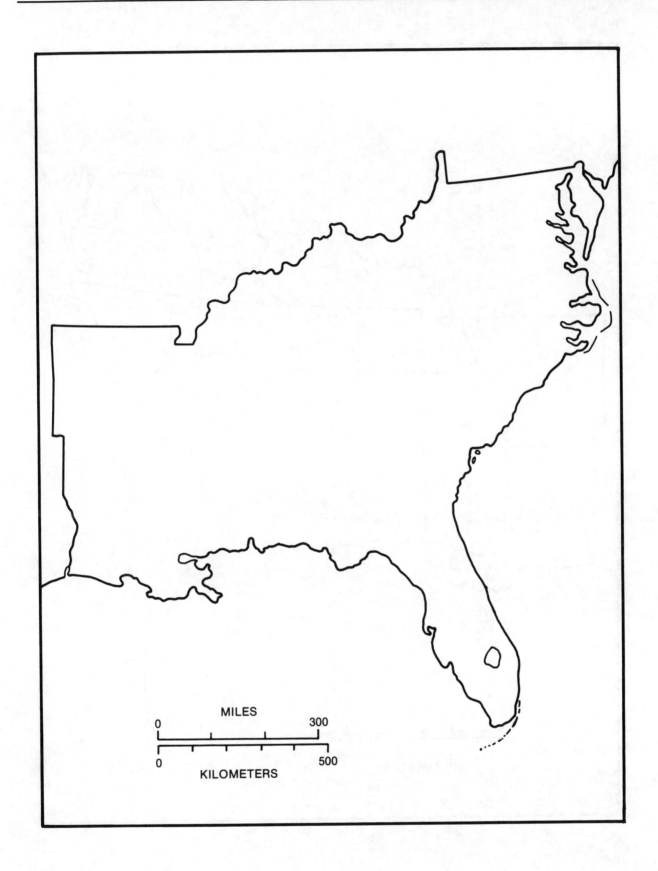

MILES

0   300

0   500

KILOMETERS

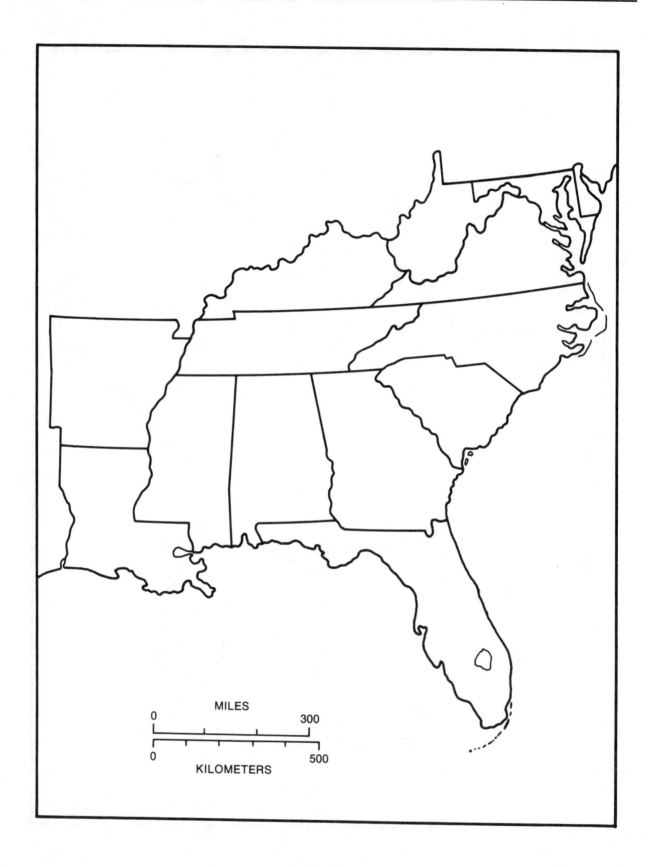

MILES

0   300

0   500

KILOMETERS

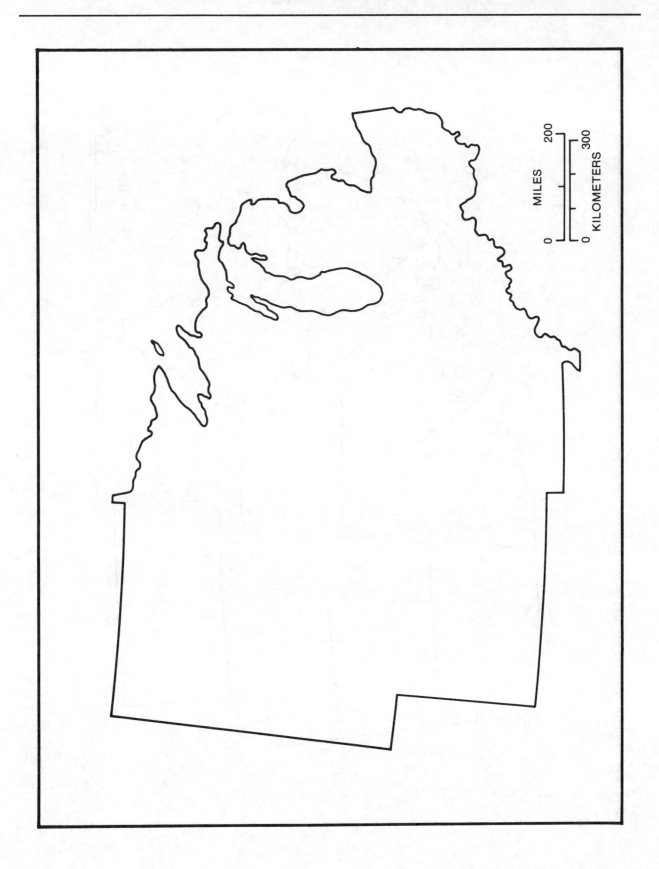

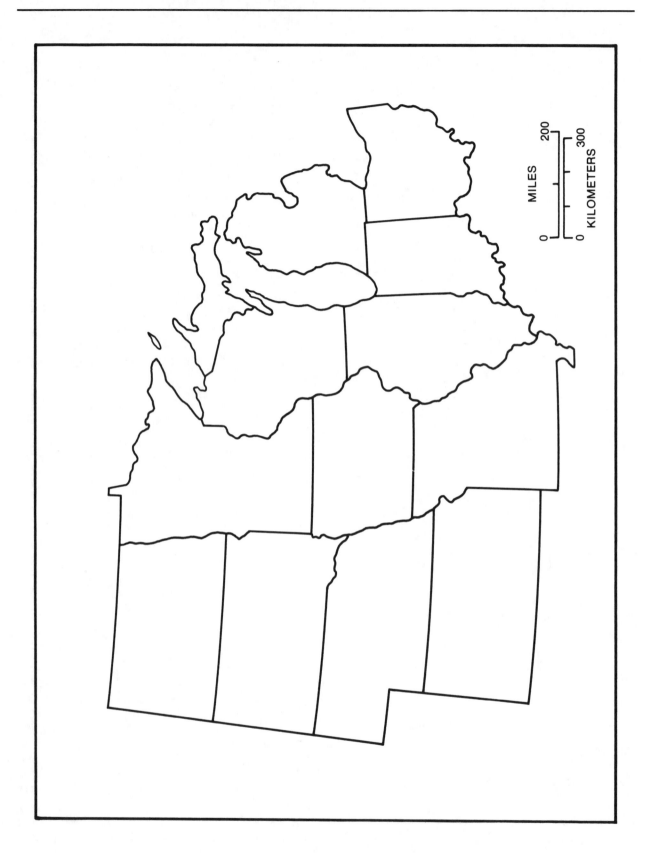

MILES

200

KILOMETERS

300

0

0

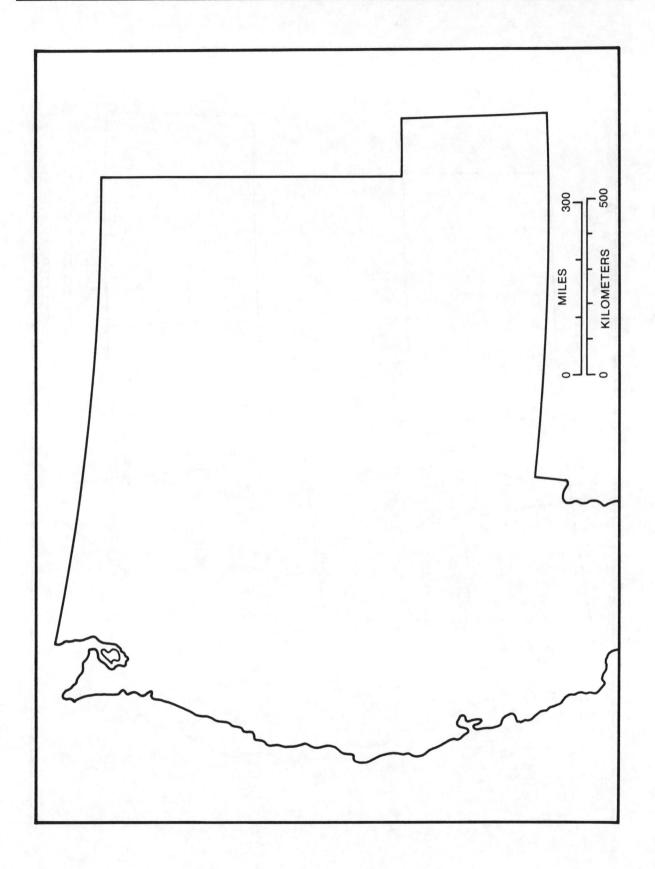

MILES

KILOMETERS

300

500

0

0

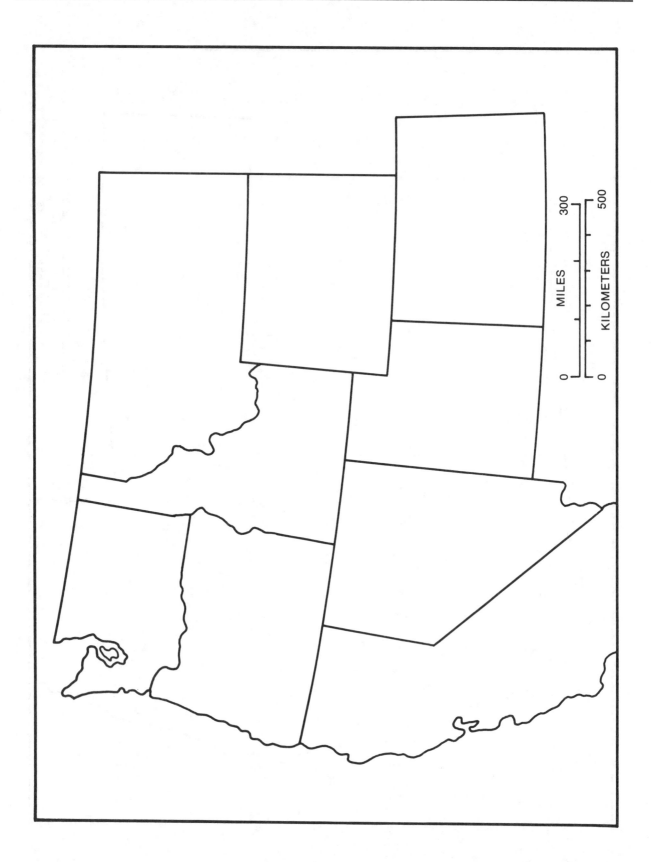

MILES

300

KILOMETERS

500

0

0

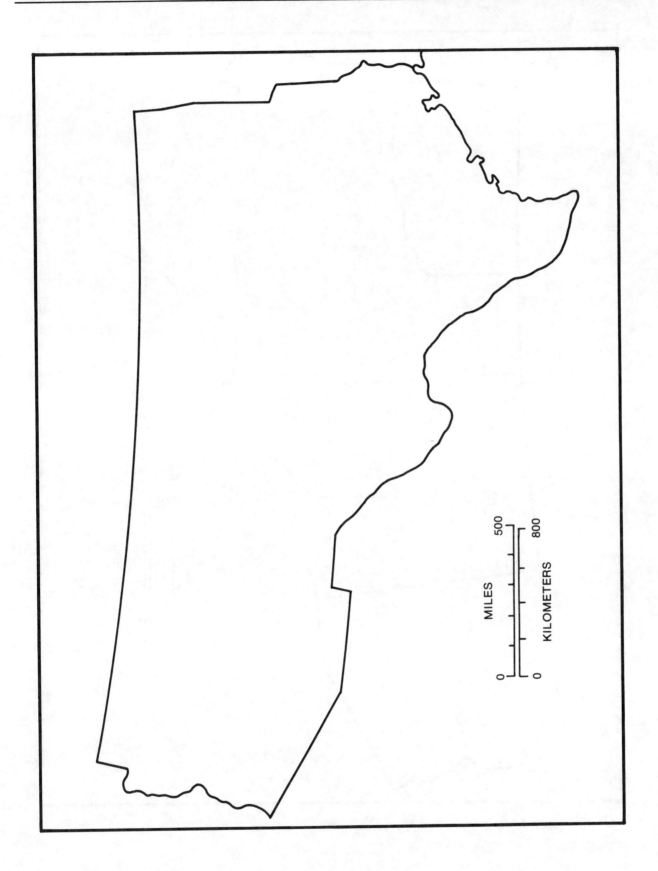

MILES

KILOMETERS

500

800

0

0

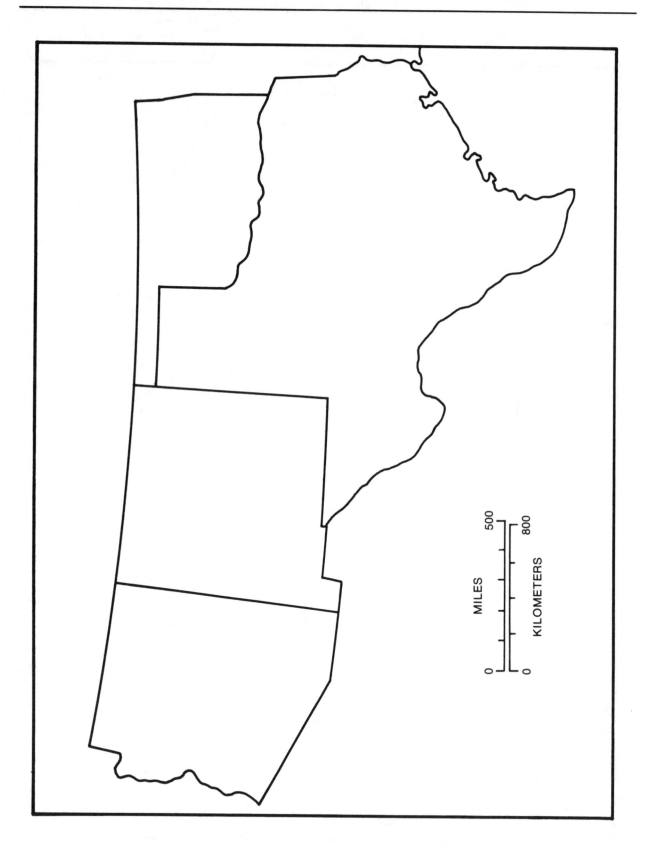

MILES

500

KILOMETERS

800

0

0

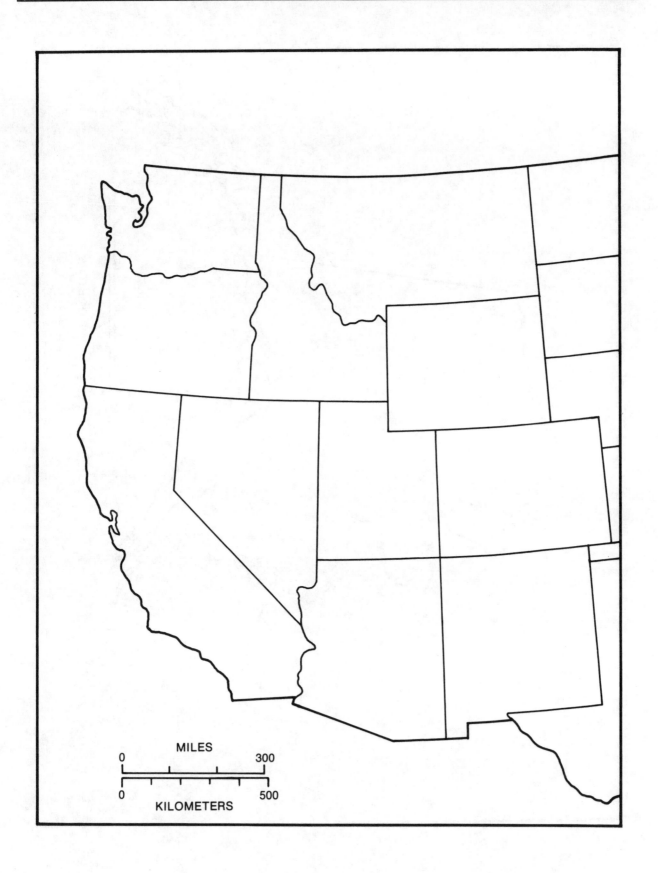

MILES

0   300

0   500

KILOMETERS

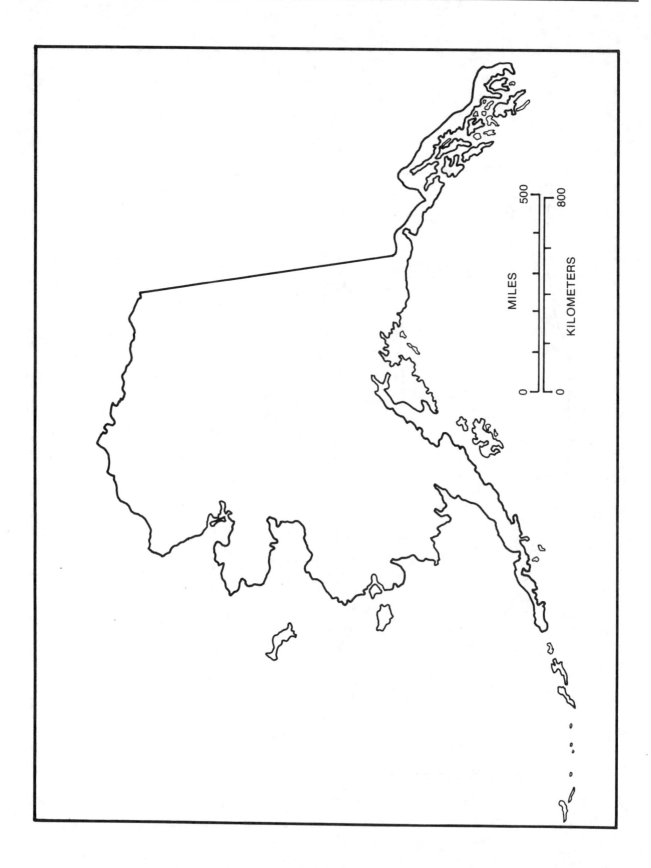

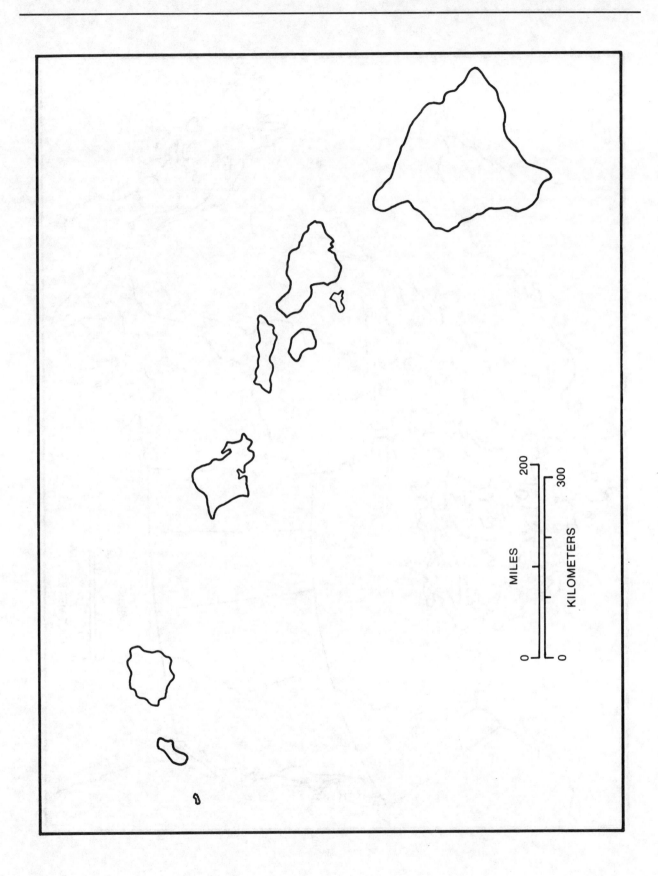

MILES

KILOMETERS

200

300

0

0

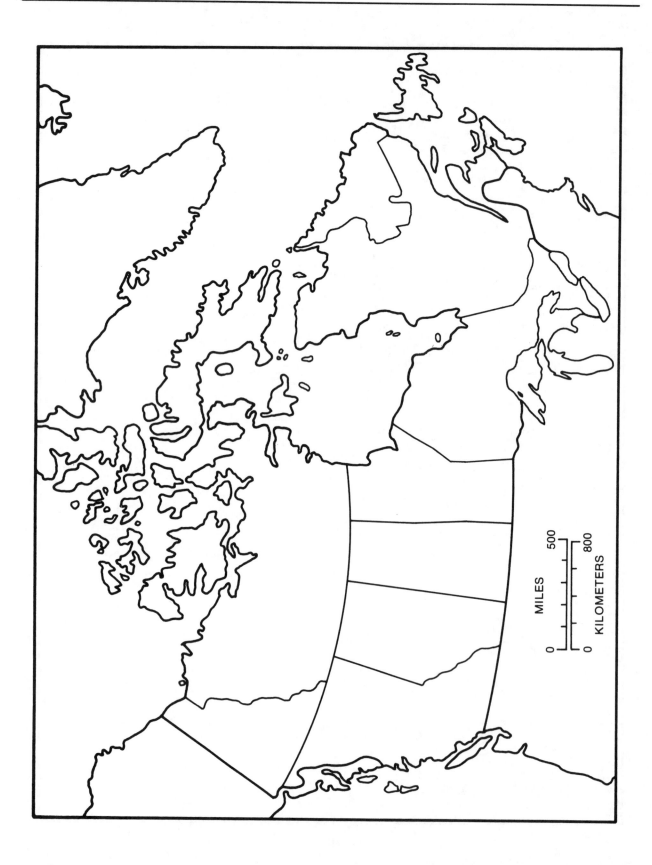

MILES

500

0

KILOMETERS

800

0

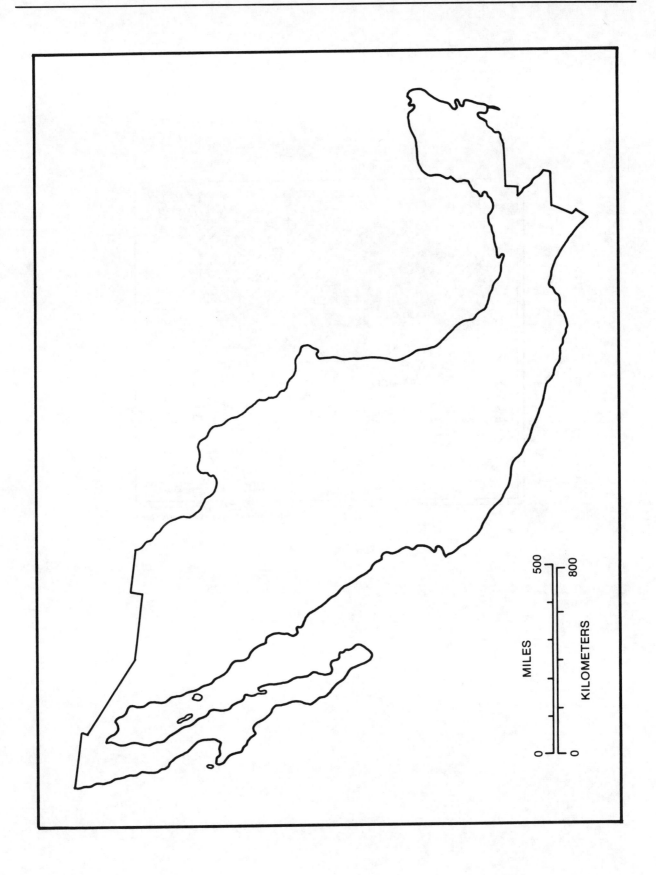

MILES

KILOMETERS

500

800

0

0

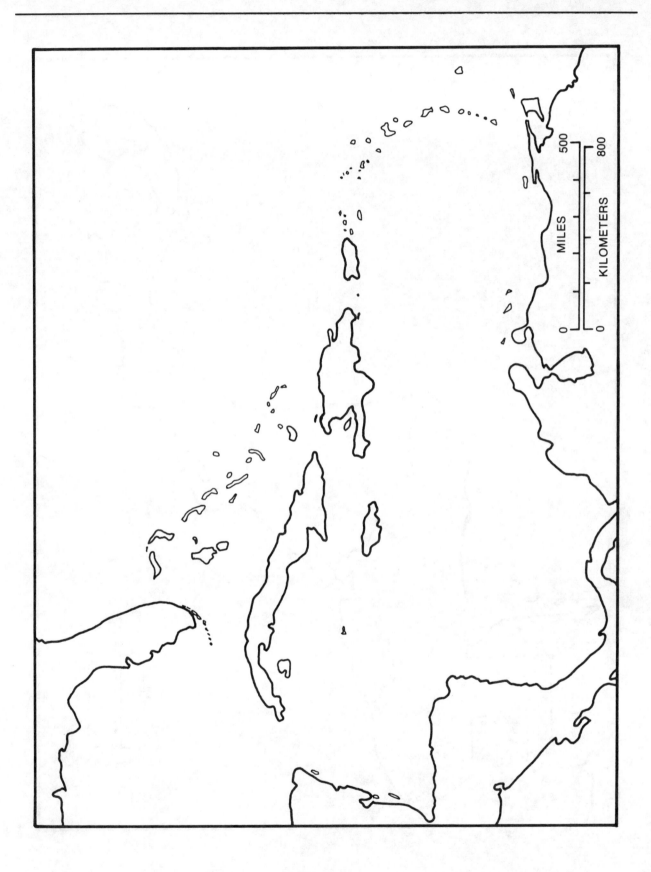

MILES

KILOMETERS

500

800

0

0

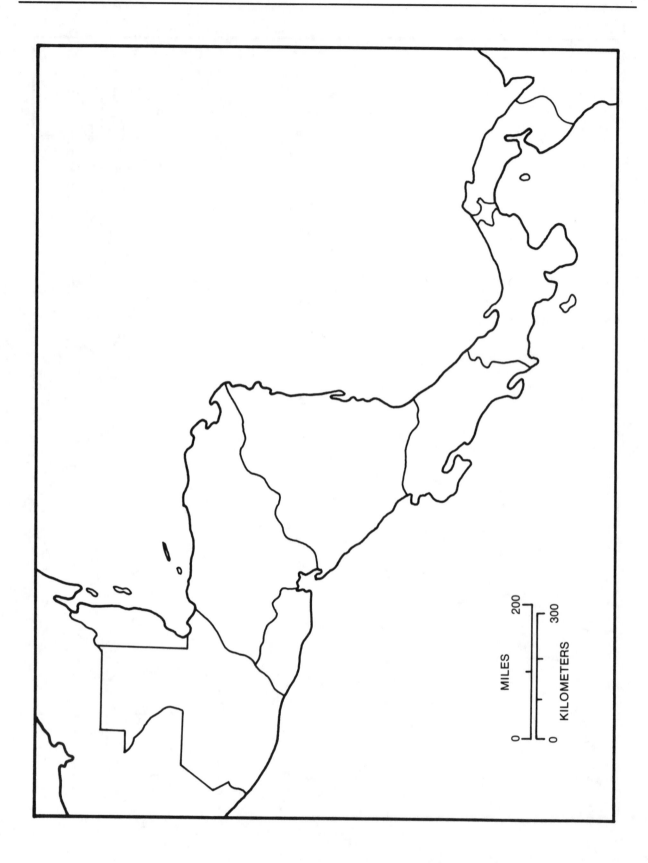

MILES

KILOMETERS

200

300

0

0

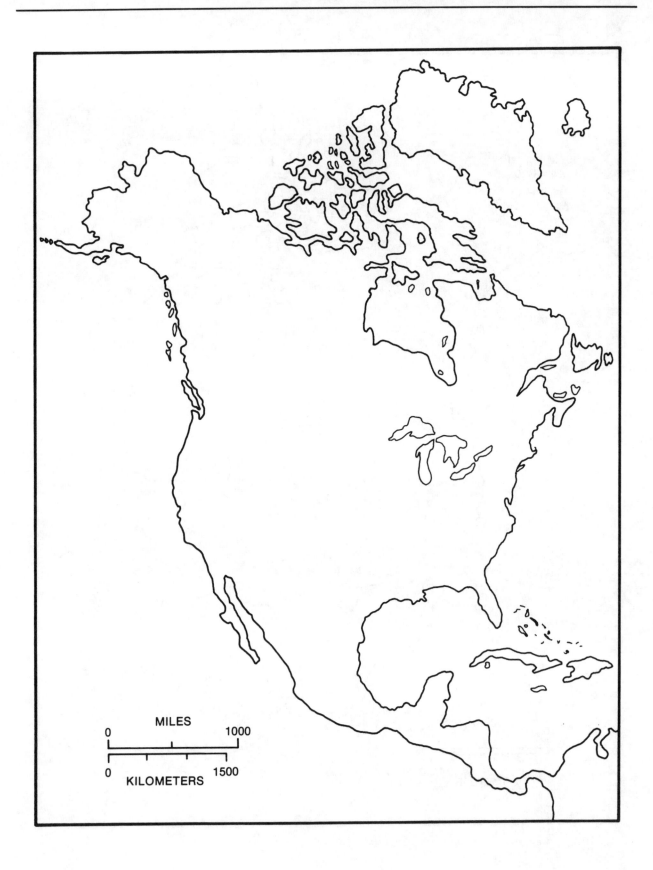

MILES

0   1000

0   1500

KILOMETERS

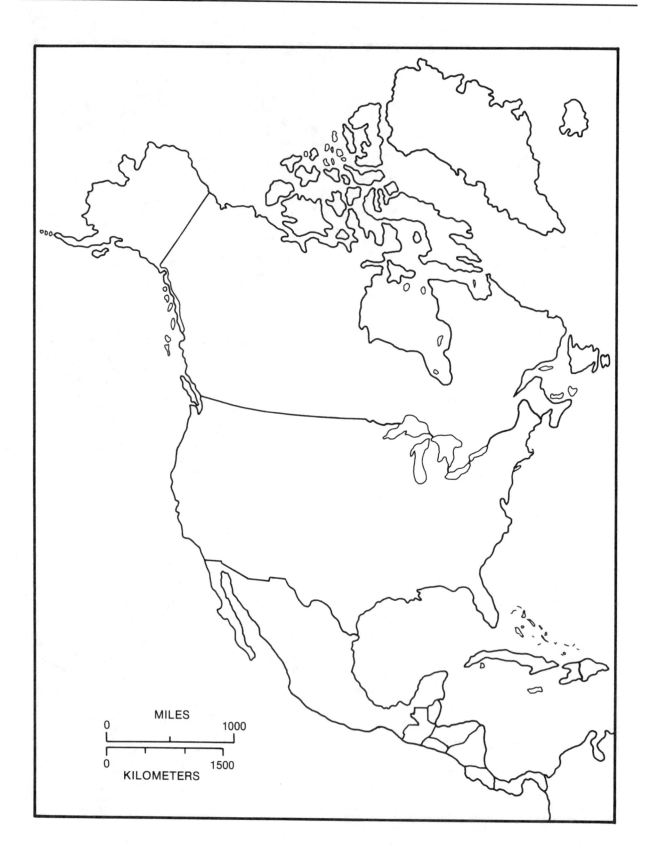

MILES

0   1000

0   1500

KILOMETERS

MILES

0   500

0   800

KILOMETERS

MILES

0   500

0   800

KILOMETERS

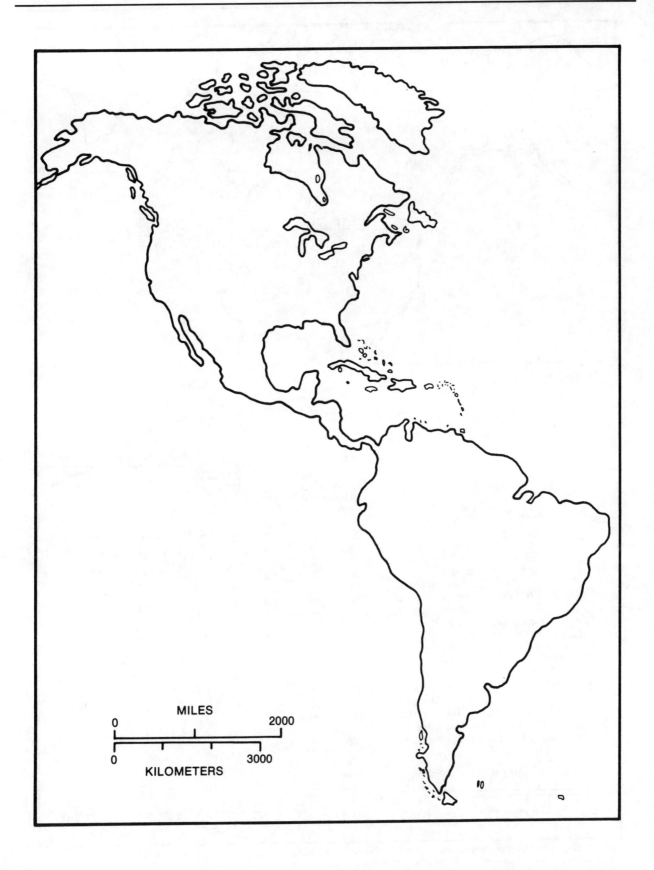

MILES

0   2000

0   3000

KILOMETERS

Appendix Map 30. Bird Migration Routes

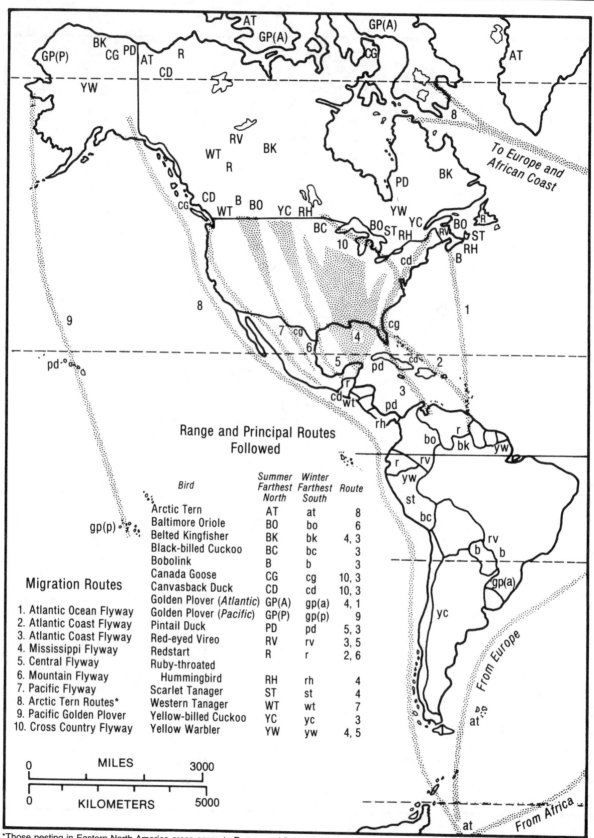

Range and Principal Routes Followed

Bird	Summer Farthest North	Winter Farthest South	Route
Arctic Tern	AT	at	8
Baltimore Oriole	BO	bo	6
Belted Kingfisher	BK	bk	4, 3
Black-billed Cuckoo	BC	bc	3
Bobolink	B	b	3
Canada Goose	CG	cg	10, 3
Canvasback Duck	CD	cd	10, 3
Golden Plover (*Atlantic*)	GP(A)	gp(a)	4, 1
Golden Plover (*Pacific*)	GP(P)	gp(p)	9
Pintail Duck	PD	pd	5, 3
Red-eyed Vireo	RV	rv	3, 5
Redstart	R	r	2, 6
Ruby-throated Hummingbird	RH	rh	4
Scarlet Tanager	ST	st	4
Western Tanager	WT	wt	7
Yellow-billed Cuckoo	YC	yc	3
Yellow Warbler	YW	yw	4, 5

Migration Routes

1. Atlantic Ocean Flyway
2. Atlantic Coast Flyway
3. Atlantic Coast Flyway
4. Mississippi Flyway
5. Central Flyway
6. Mountain Flyway
7. Pacific Flyway
8. Arctic Tern Routes*
9. Pacific Golden Plover
10. Cross Country Flyway

MILES 0 — 3000

KILOMETERS 0 — 5000

*Those nesting in Eastern North America cross ocean to Europe and fly south along African coast and across south Atlantic. Those nesting in west follow along Pacific coast of North and South America.

Used by permission, The National Audubon Society.

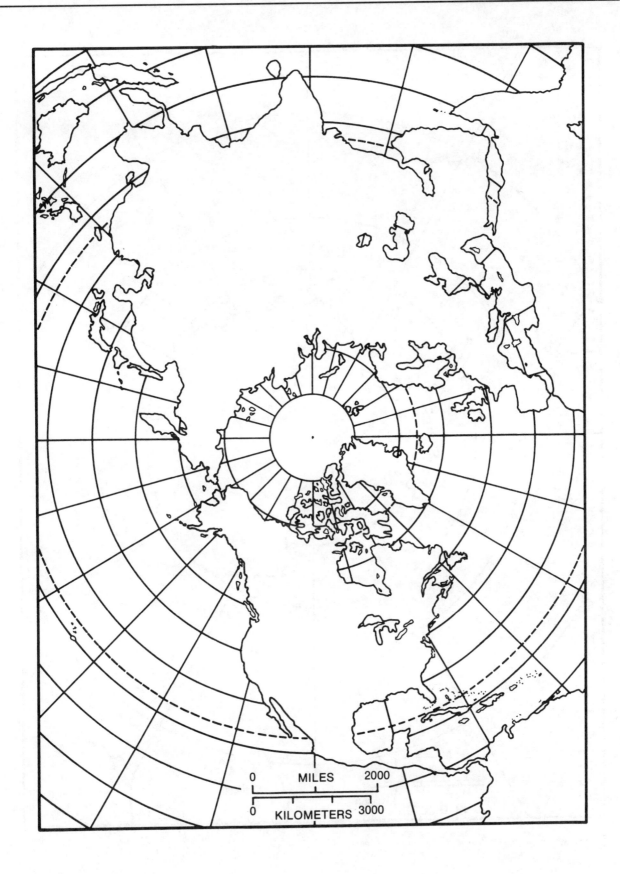

0   MILES   2000

0   KILOMETERS   3000

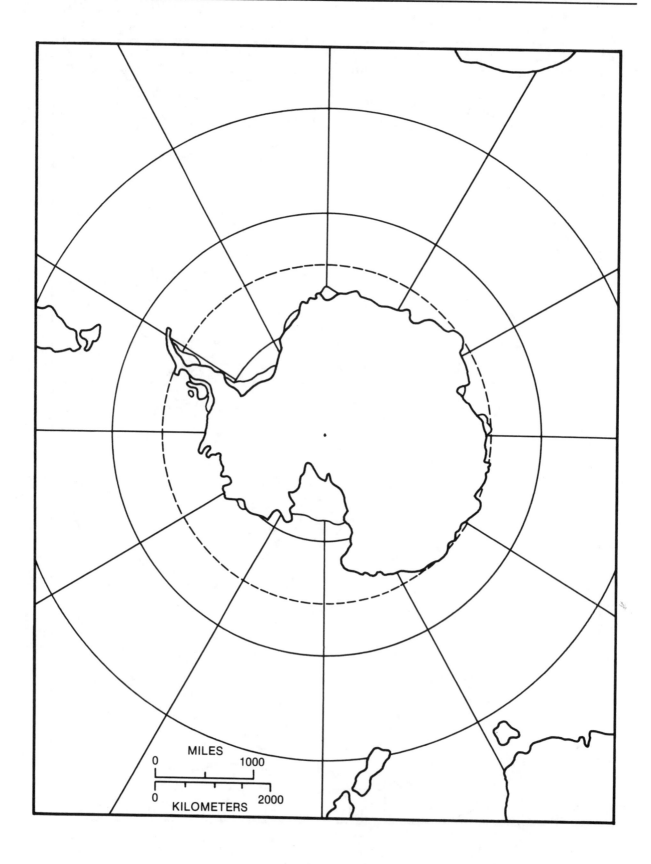

MILES

0   1000

0   2000
KILOMETERS

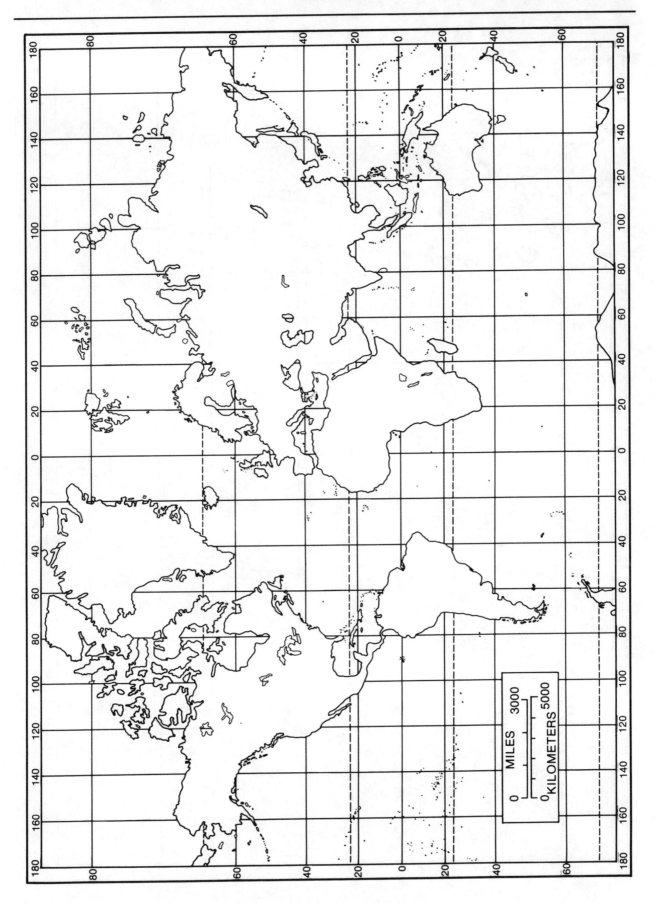

111

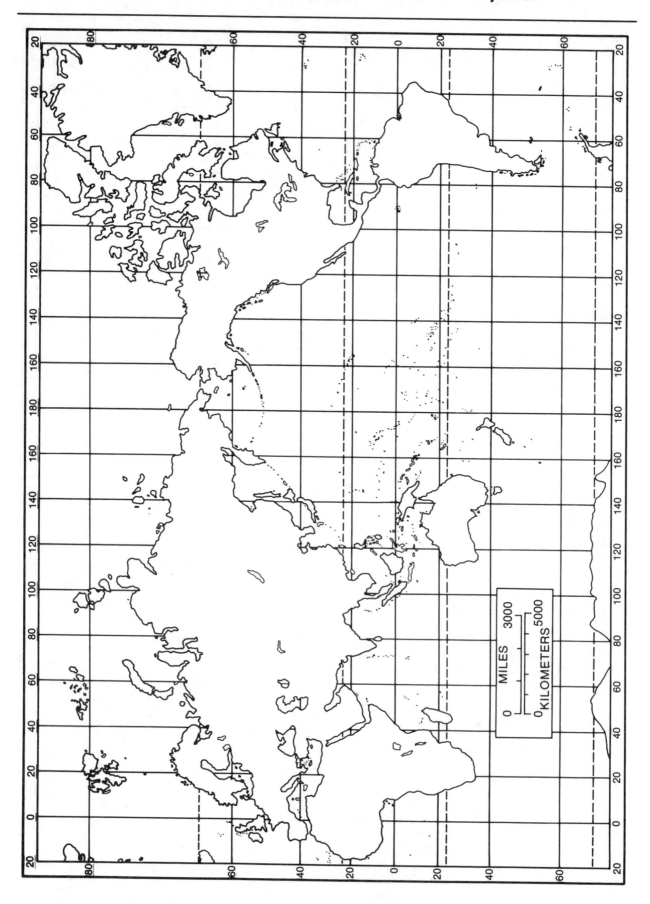

MILES 3000
KILOMETERS 5000

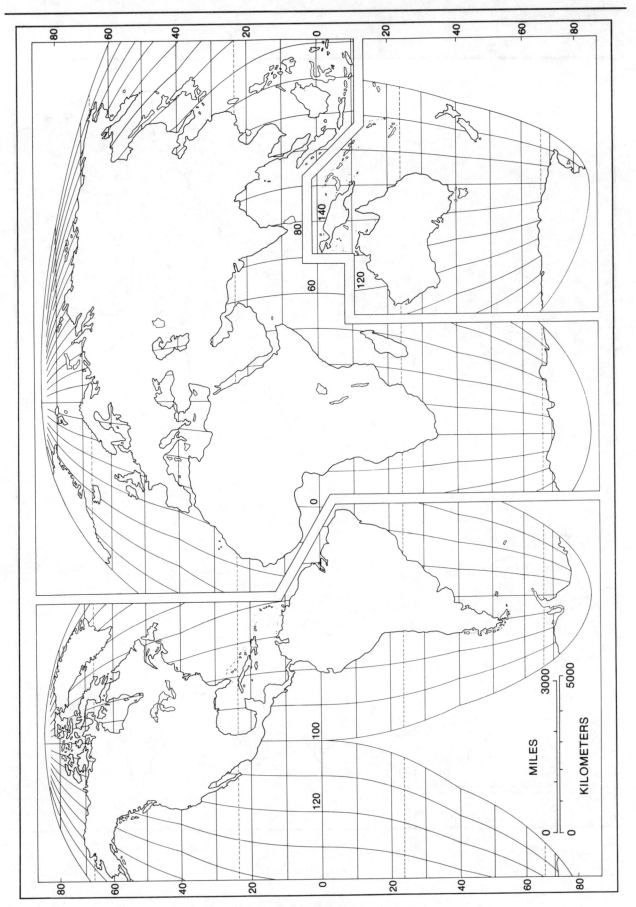

MILES

KILOMETERS

113

MILES

0   500

0   800

KILOMETERS

MILES

0   500

0   800

KILOMETERS

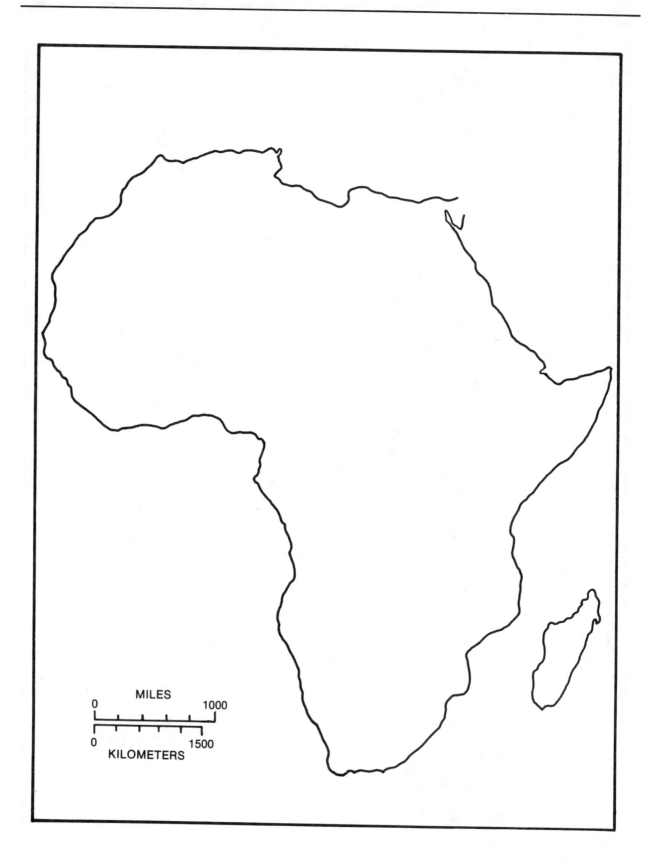

MILES

0   1000

0   1500

KILOMETERS

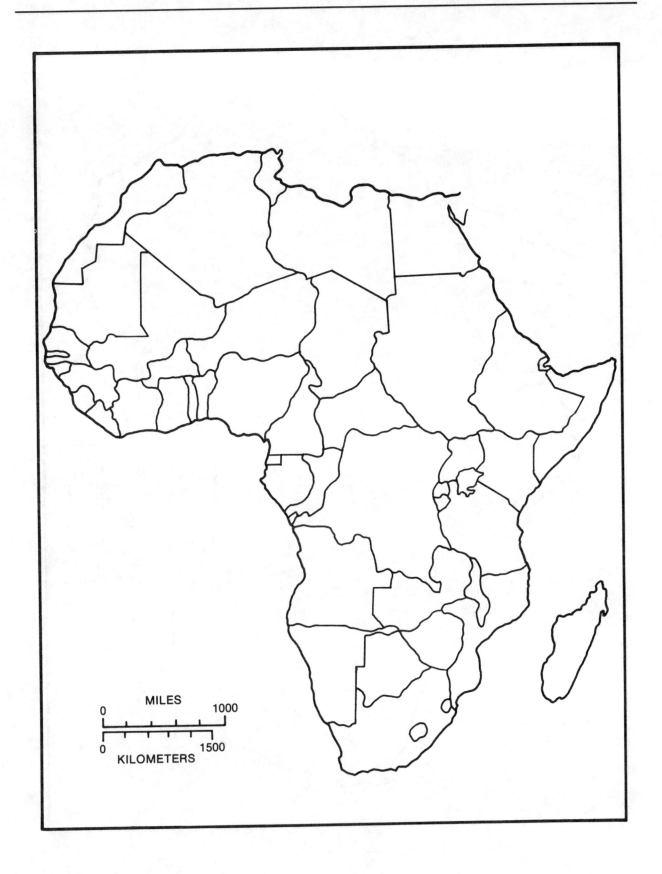

MILES

0   1000

0   1500
KILOMETERS

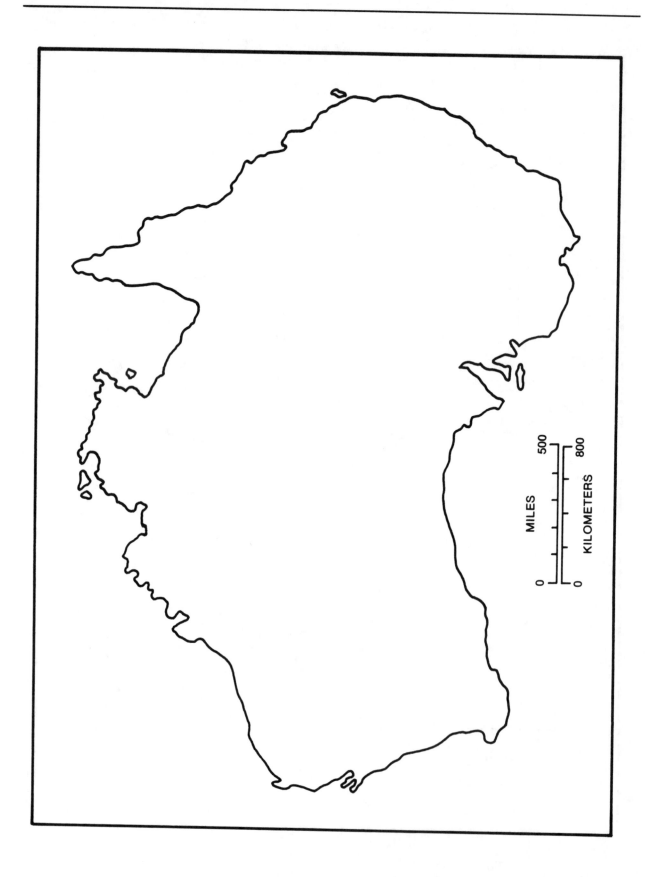

MILES

KILOMETERS

500

800

0

0

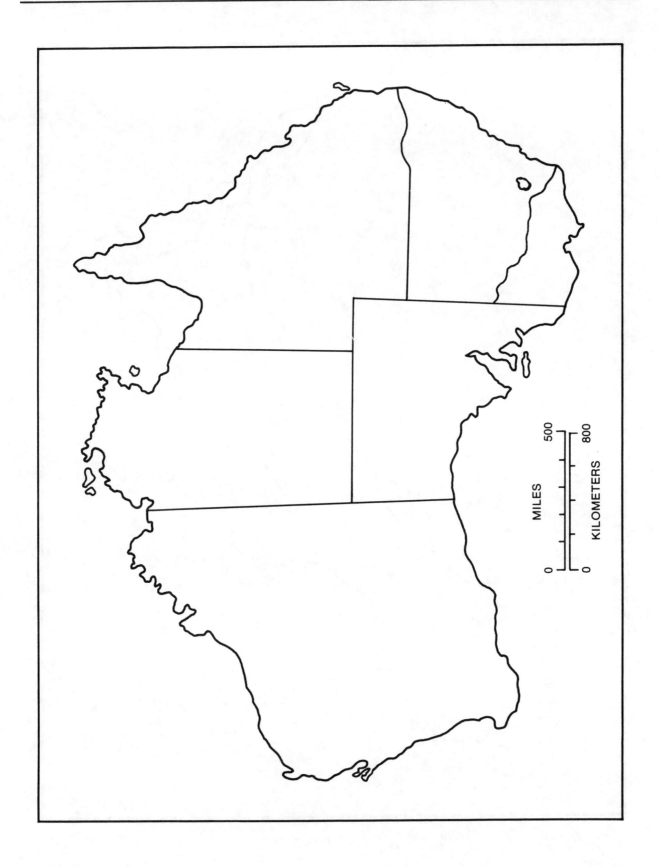

MILES

500

KILOMETERS

800

0

0

119

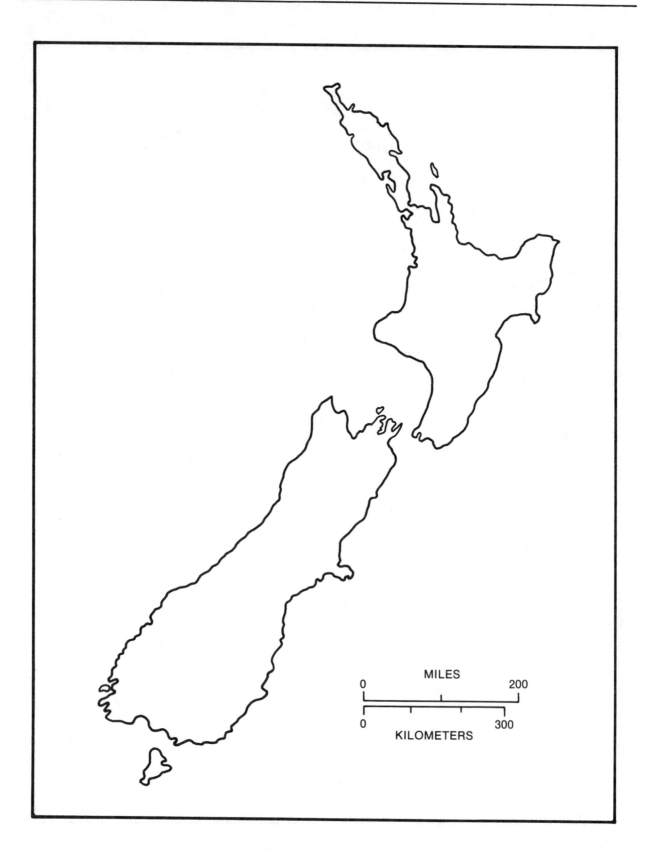

MILES

0   200

0   300

KILOMETERS

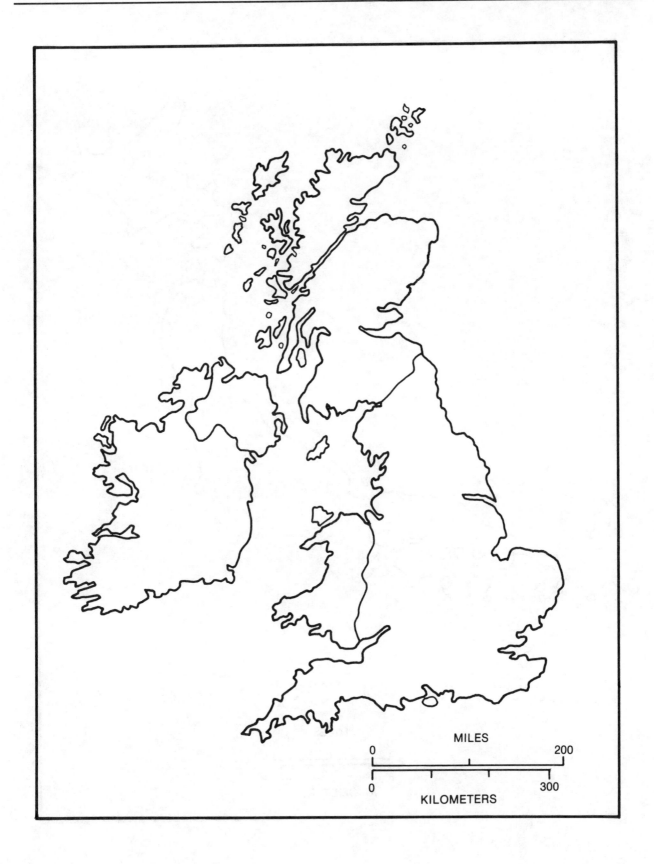

MILES

0   200

0   300

KILOMETERS

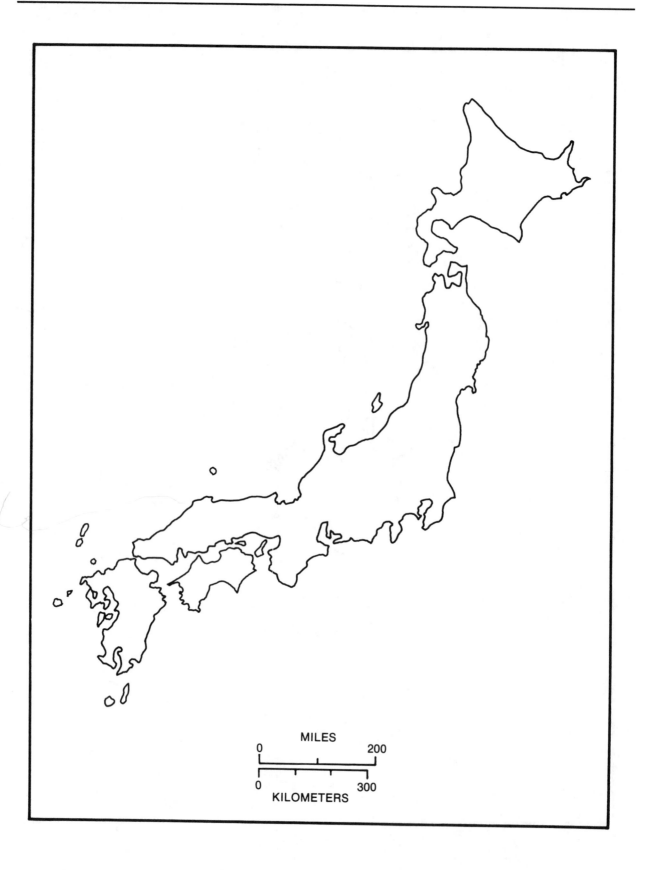

MILES

0   200

0   300

KILOMETERS

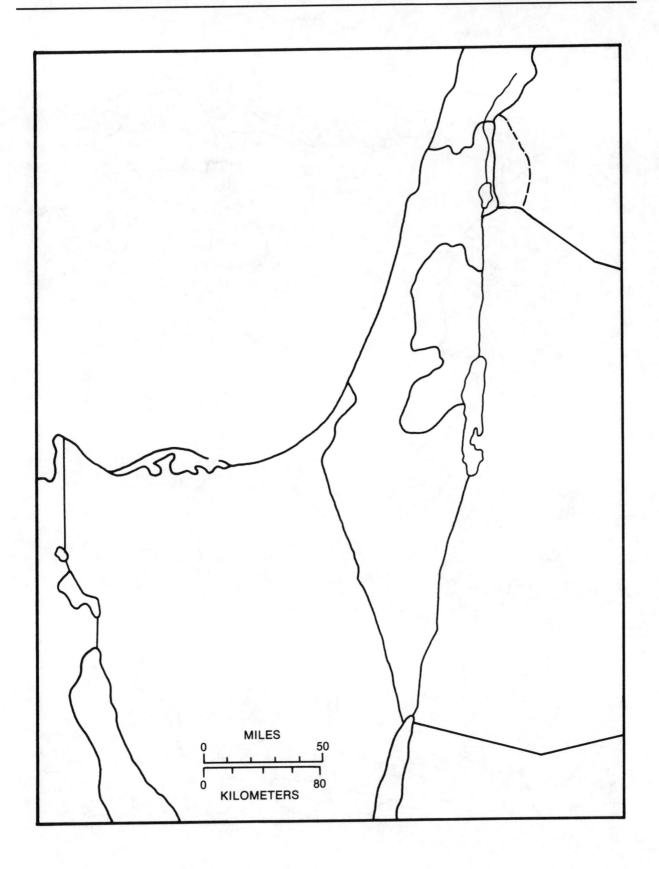

MILES

0   50

0   80
KILOMETERS

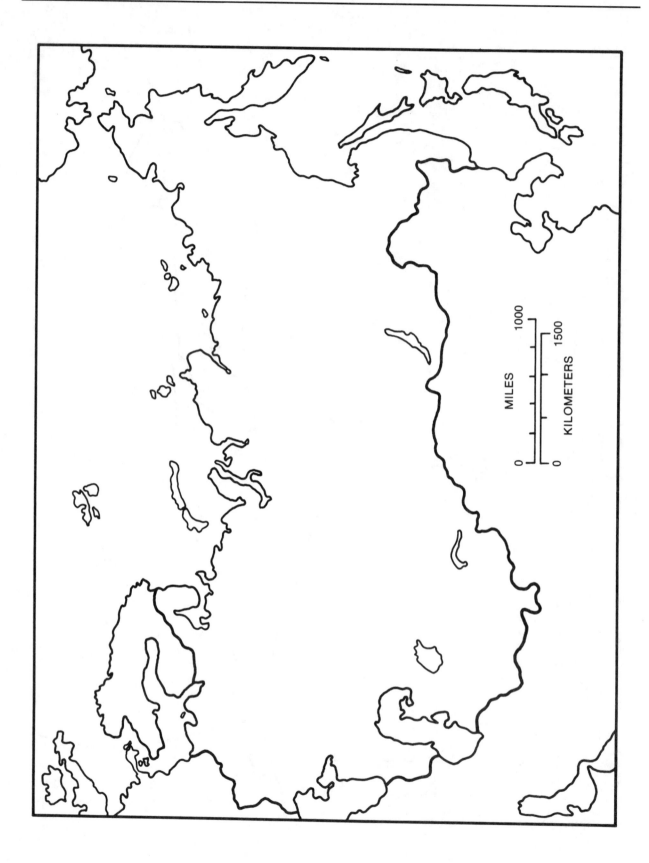

MILES

1000

0

KILOMETERS

1500

0

124

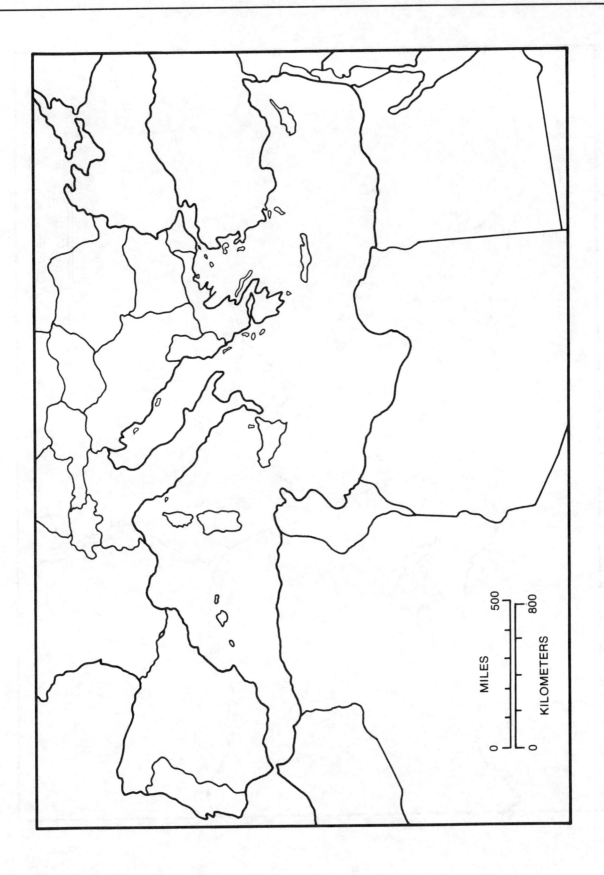

MILES

KILOMETERS

500

800

0

0

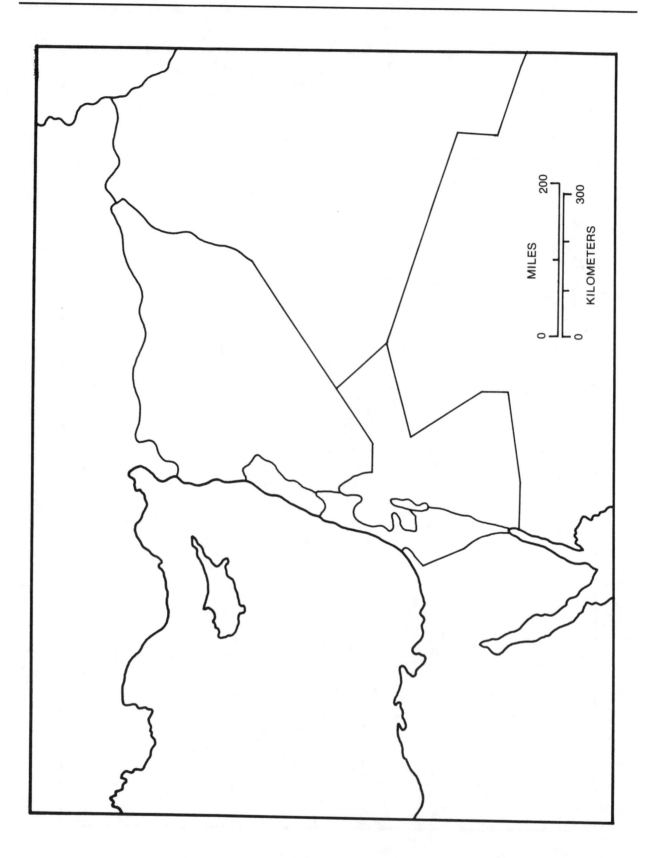

MILES

200

KILOMETERS

300

0

0

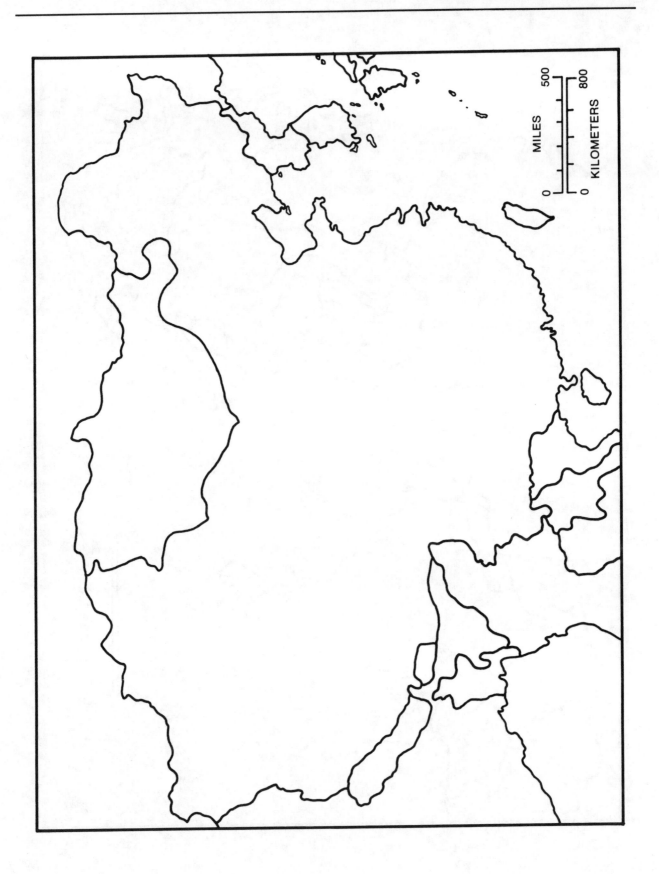

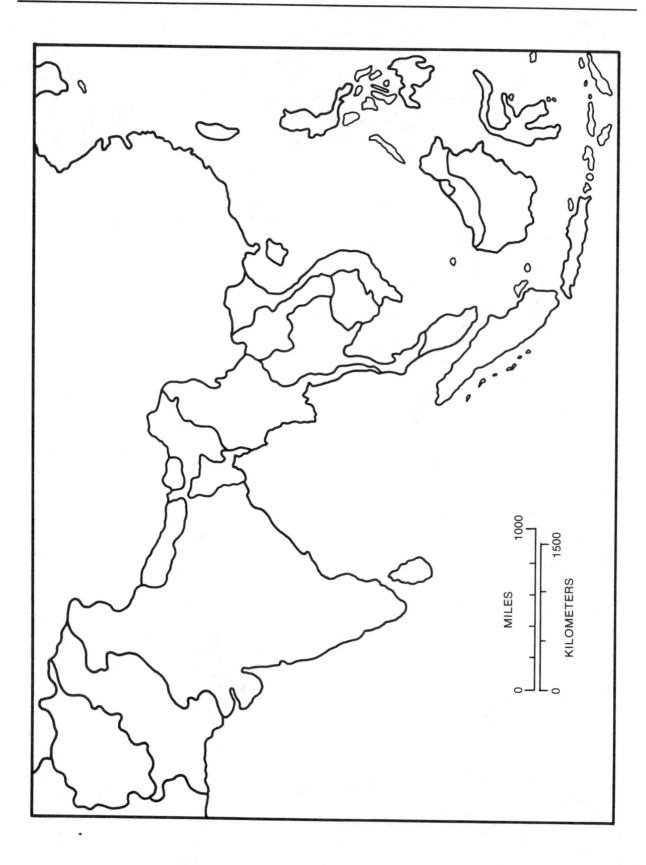

MILES

1000

KILOMETERS

1500

0

0